SUGAR CREEK GANG
THE THOUSAND DOLLAR FISH

Original title:
North Woods Manhunt

Paul Hutchens

MOODY PRESS • CHICAGO

ISBN 0-8024-4815-1

23 25 27 29 30 28 26 24 22

Printed in the United States of America

1

I TELL YOU, when you just *know* there's going to be some exciting trouble in the next twelve minutes or less, you have to make your red head do some quick clear thinking, if you can.

Not a one of the Sugar Creek Gang knew *what* was going to happen, but the very minute I heard that outboard motor roaring out on the lake, the sound sounding like it was coming straight toward the shore and the old icehouse we were all in, I said to us, "Quick, Gang! Let's get out of here and get this ransom money back to camp!"

Little Jim's gunny sack had a lot of money in it right that minute, which we'd dug up out of the sawdust in that abandoned old icehouse. The gunny sack was nearly filled with stuffed fish, the big and middle-sized northern and walleyed pike, with thousands and thousands of dollars sewed up inside.

I won't take time right now to tell you all you maybe ought to know about how we happened to find that ransom money buried in the saw-

5

dust of that old icehouse, 'cause that'd take too long, and besides you've probably read all about it in the last story about the Sugar Creek Gang, which is called *Sugar Creek Gang Digs for Treasure*. I had better tell you, though, that a little St. Paul girl named Marie Ostberg had been kidnapped and the kidnapper had hidden up in the Chippewa forest of northern Minnesota in what is called "The Paul Bunyan Country," where we were camping. Our gang had found the girl in the middle of the night and captured the kidnapper in an old Indian cemetery the next night. Then we had a very mysterious and exciting time hunting for the ransom money in one of the strangest places in all the world to find money. At last we found it in this very old icehouse, and, as I told you, the money had been sewed up inside of these great big fish which we'd been digging up and stuffing into the gunny sack.

In maybe another seven minutes we'd have had it all dug up and stuffed into the gunny sack and would have been on our way back to camp. But all of a startling sudden we heard that outboard motor roaring in our direction from out on the lake and we knew that unless we stepped on the gas, we would never be able to get out of the opening and far enough away in the bushes not to be seen.

"What's the sense of being scared?" Dragonfly, the popeyed member of our gang, asked me right after I'd ordered us all to get going quick. "The kidnapper's caught and in jail, isn't he?"

"Sure, but Old hook-nosed John Till's running loose up here somewhere," I said. Old Hook-nose was a very fierce man and the unpleasant infidel dad of one of the members of our gang. He had been in jail a lot of times in his wicked life and was staying in a cabin not more than a quarter of a mile up the shore from where we were right that minute.

Poetry, the barrel-shaped member of the gang, who knew one hundred and one poems by heart and was always quoting one, swished around quick, scrambled back across the sawdust we'd been digging in, peeped through a crack between the logs toward the lake.

"Who *is* it?" I said, and he said in his duck-like squawky voice, "I can't tell, but he looks awful mad."

Well, anybody knows nobody could see well enough that far to see a person's face well enough to tell whether it had a mad look on it. But if it was John Till who hated us boys anyway, he'd probably be mad and would do savage things to all of us, if he caught us in that icehouse getting the money.

7

So in another six or seven jiffies we were all scrambling as fast as we could *out* of that icehouse and out into the open, carrying Little Jim's gunny sack full of fish. We made a dive across an open space to a clump of bushes, where we wouldn't be seen by anybody on the lake.

Circus, the acrobatic member of our gang, was with us too, and he, being the strongest one of us, grabbed up the sack, swung it over his shoulder and loped on ahead of us. "Hurry!" we panted to each other, and didn't stop running until we reached the top of a hill, which we did just as we heard the outboard motor stop. There we all dropped down on the grass, gasping and panting, and tickled that we were safe. But I was feeling pretty bad to think that there were probably a half dozen other fish still buried in the sawdust in that old log icehouse.

"Quick, Poetry, give me your knife," Circus ordered.

"What for?" Poetry said, and at the same time shoved his fat hand in his pocket and pulled out his official boy-scout knife. He handed it over to Circus, who quick opened the heavy cutting blade and started ripping open the sewed-up stomach of a big northern pike which he'd just pulled out of the sack.

8

"There's no sense in carrying home a six-pound northern pike with only a quarter of a pound of twenty-dollar bills in it," Circus said. I knew he was right, 'cause it was a long way back to our camp, and if for any reason we had to run fast, we could do it better without having to lug along those great big fish, especially the biggest one.

I didn't bother to watch Circus though, 'cause right that second I started peering through the foliage of some oak undergrowth back toward the lake, just as I saw a man come swishing around the corner of the icehouse and stop in front of the opened door.

"Hey *look!*" Dragonfly said to us. "He's got a big string of big fish."

And sure enough he had.

Little Jim, who was beside me, holding onto his stick which he always carried with him when we were on a hike or out in the woods, whispered close to my ear, "I'll bet he's got a lot more money sewed up in a lot more fish, and is going to bury it in the sawdust where these were."

I happened to have my high-powered binoculars with me so I quick unsnapped the carrying case they were in, zipped them out, raised them to my eyes and right away it seemed like I was only about one-third as far away as I was. I gasped so loud

9

at what I saw—or rather *whom* I saw—that my gasp was almost like a yell.

"SH!" Circus said to us, just like he was the leader of our gang, which he wasn't. I was leader—that is, I was *supposed* to be, 'cause our real leader, Big Jim, wasn't with us, but was back at camp with Little Tom Till, the newest member of our gang.

"It's Old Hook-nose, all right," I said, and knew it was. I could see his stoop-shoulders, dark complexion, red hair, bulgy eyes, bushy eyebrows, and his hook nose.

"What if he finds we've dug up part of the fish and run away with them?" Little Jim asked in a half-scared voice.

"Maybe he won't," I said, and hoped he wouldn't.

While I was watching John Till toss his stringer of fish up into the opening and clamber up after them, Circus was slashing open the fish and taking out the ransom money which was folded in nice flat packets of wax paper like the kind my mom uses in our kitchen back home at Sugar Creek.

We also all helped Circus do what he was doing, all of us maybe more excited than we'd been in a long time, while different ones of us took turns watching what Hook-nose was doing.

I knew that in only a few jiffies he would be out of that icehouse again, and probably would go back to the big white boat he'd come to shore in, shove off and row out a few feet. And then there would be a roar of his motor and away he would go swishing out across the sunlit water, his boat making a long widening V behind him. Then we would sneak back and get the rest of the money.

Everything was pretty clear in my mind as to what had been going on the last day or two. Perhaps John Till had been what police call an "accomplice" of the real kidnapper and it had been his special job to look after the ransom money. He'd decided that the best way in the world to hide it where nobody would ever think of finding it would be to catch some big fish, cut them open, clean out the entrails, fold the money in packets of wax paper, stuff it inside the fish, and sew it up, like my mother sews up a chicken she's stuffed with dressing just before she slides it into the oven for our dinner. Then he would dig down deep in the sawdust of the icehouse till he came to some ice, lay the fish on it, and cover it up. Nobody would ever think to look inside a fish for money. Even if they accidentally dug up a fish, it'd be covered with wettish

11

sticky sawdust, and they wouldn't see the stitches in its stomach.

Say, while I was thinking that and also watching the shadow of John Till through the door of the icehouse, all of a sudden there was a quick gasp beside me. I said to Circus, "What on earth?" thinking maybe he'd found something terribly special, but he hadn't. He dropped his knife, leaped to his feet, and said, "You guys stay here! I'll be right back."

"Stop!" I said. "Where are you going?" I remembered I was supposed to be the leader, but Circus had his own ideas about that. He squirmed out of my grasp, almost tearing his shirt because I had hold of it and didn't want to let go.

The next second there were only four of us left—barrel-shaped Poetry, kind-faced, swell Little Jim, pop-eyed Dragonfly, and me, red-haired, fiery-tempered, freckle-faced Bill Collins. Circus, our acrobat, was streaking out through the bushes as fast as he could go toward the lake and the icehouse, but not getting out in the open where John could see him.

"What on earth?" I thought. I didn't dare yell, or try to stop him by whistling or something, or John Till would have heard me, and who knows what might have happened? I didn't have the slightest idea what Circus was up to until a moment later, when I saw him dart like a scared chipmunk out from some bushes not far from the icehouse and make a dive for the open door.

"Why the crazy goof!" I thought. "He's going to try to—" What *was* he going to try to do?

I soon found out. It happened so fast, I didn't even have time to think.

SWISH! Wham! A half-dozen flying movements, and it was all over. Circus grabbed that icehouse door, swung it shut, lifted the big heavy bar and threw it into place, and Old hook-nosed John Till was locked inside!

2

Circus hadn't any more than slammed that ice-house door shut and dropped the heavy bar into place, locking Old Hook-nose in, than there was a loud pounding on the door and a yelling that sounded like there was a madman inside.

What on earth to do next was the question. We were an awful long way from camp, and we five young boys certainly weren't big enough to capture him ourselves. Besides yesterday when we'd first seen him, he'd had a big hunting knife and who knows but he might have a gun too. Anybody as fierce and as mad as John Till was right that minute—well, you couldn't tell what he might do, if he got a chance.

Circus was coming in our direction now as fast as he could, and when a few jiffies later he came puffing up to us, he exclaimed, "Come on, Gang. Let's run back to camp and get help."

And right that minute I got a bright idea of my own. In fact it had been swishing around in my mind ever since I'd seen Circus wham that

15

door shut. I said, "Come on, Gang. Follow me and we'll get help in a hurry."

I grabbed up the gunny sack which had the rest of the stuffed fish in it and the packets of the ransom money, and it felt as light as a feather as I started on a fast dash right straight toward the icehouse again.

"Hey, where are you going?" Poetry hissed and yelled to me at the same time.

"Back to camp," I said. "Come on!"

"Camp's in this other direction," Dragonfly called after me.

"Do as I say," I yelled back over my shoulder, and kept on running like a deer straight for the icehouse.

It felt good to realize that all the gang was coming swishing along after me, that I was actually the leader—for awhile anyway. I had what I thought was a swell idea. My dad once told me what happens to a person when he becomes a leader. First he gets an idea about something which he thinks is wonderful, and which ought to be done, and right away he starts getting a lot of people to help him do it.

You see, while Circus was slamming that door and shutting Old Hook-nose inside, and I was watching him with my binoculars, I'd seen John's white boat which was beached there at the lake and had noticed that the outboard motor, which was tilted forward in the stern, had a beautiful black shroud. It was the same kind our camp director had, and I'd been learning how to run it during the past week. It had a powerful seven-horsepower motor and could go terribly fast on a lake. If there is something I'd rather do than anything else, it is to sit in the stern of a boat, with one hand on the rubber grip of the steering handle, and, facing the prow, go roaring out across the water with fast wind blowing into my freckled face and also feel the shoreline flash past very fast.

I also knew that the water in many of the big blue-watered lakes up here in the North was kept fresh because the Mississippi river flowed through them, and also flowed from one lake to another. I'd studied the map of the territory and knew that if we could use that boat and motor, we could go roaring up the lake terribly fast, pass the old Indian cemetery in three or four minutes, and a little later, come to a place where the Mississippi flowed out of this lake into a long narrow channel and into the other very large lake on which we had our tents pitched. Once we got into that other lake we'd race up the shore, and get back to camp in less than half the time it

17

would take us to hike through the woods, carrying a big heavy sack of fish.

We could leave John Till locked up in the icehouse while we were gone, and hurry back with Big Jim and maybe some other help, and before long we'd have John Till *really* captured. After that, we'd tell the police what we'd done, then we could claim the reward for finding the thousands and thousands of dollars which the little Ostberg girl's dad had paid to the kidnapper.

In a minute I was hurrying past the icehouse with my gunny sack of fish. I stopped for a split-jiffy to listen, but everything was pretty quiet. I noticed that the heavy door was really strong and I didn't see any way John Till could get out. There also was only one place where he could even *see* out and that was through a crack on the side next to the lake.

In a jiffy all of us were in the boat, and had shoved off and rowed out to deep enough water to make it safe to start the motor without its propeller striking on the bottom.

I was pretty nervous, and also scared and brave at the same time. It wasn't our boat or motor, but we weren't stealing it. We were amateur detectives using the criminal's boat to get some help to capture him.

It was a real pretty sunshiny day, with only

18

a few scattered white clouds in the sky. In another minute we'd be gone. Poetry was in the middle, on a seat by himself, Dragonfly and Little Jim in one right in front of me, and Circus had a narrow seat up in the prow.

"I don't see why you don't let *me* run it," Poetry complained. "After all, I taught you how to run it in the first place."

"SH!" I said. "Can't you cooperate?" That is a word my dad sometimes uses back at Sugar Creek when he wants me to obey him. "You keep your eye on the gunny sack there between your feet."

I quick opened the gasoline shut-off valve as far as it would turn, being sure first that the air vent on the tank was open, shoved the speed control lever over to where it said "Start," primed the motor, and gave the starter knob a very fast sharp pull. In a jiffy that powerful motor roared itself to life and our boat went whizzing up the lake. I made a couple of other quick adjustments which I knew how to do, and away we went, the wind blowing hard in our faces or against our backs, depending on which direction we were facing.

Right that second Circus yelled over the tops of the other kids' heads to me, and said, "Hey, Bill. He's yelling and screaming for us to stop."

"Let him yell," I said. "We'll give him something to yell about a little later." I shoved the speed control lever as far to the right as it would go, and our boat really shot forward, Circus's prow raised itself up partway out of the water and we went flying up the shore at a terrific rate of speed.

It had been a wonderful vacation for all of us, I thought, and yet we still had a half-dozen days before we would get into the station wagon and drive the long day and a half back to Sugar Creek. We'd had a lot of fun fishing and swimming and solving mysteries, such as finding the kidnapped little girl, capturing the kidnapper, and digging up the ransom money, a lot of which was right there in the boat with us in the stomachs of the fish we had in the gunny sack. The rest of the money was probably all sewed in the other fish which John Till had with him right that minute while he was locked up in that icehouse jail. Of course we still had to actually capture him.

Thinking that, I said to Poetry as he sat grinning in front of me—one of his fat hands holding onto the gunwale on each side—, "I'll bet Big Jim'll want to call the police and let *them* capture John."

Not a one of us liked the idea very well, and

we all said so, although we'd all had enough dangerous experiences for one vacation.

It was Little Jim's newest hobby which helped make this last story of our northern camping trip one we'd never forget as long as we lived.

This is the way his hobby got mixed up with our mystery. Our boat had just rounded a bend and was about to swish past the old Indian cemetery where we'd had so many exciting experiences, and as you maybe know, where we'd caught the kidnapper himself one spooky night, when all of a sudden Little Jim yelled out to us, "Hey, Gang, there's a whiskey bottle floating out there in the water. Let's stop and get it."

He pointed toward the shore where the cemetery was, and sure enough, there in the water was what looked like an upside-down whiskey bottle on the surface of the water.

"We don't have time to stop," I yelled to Little Jim, and didn't even bother to throttle the motor even a little bit. But say, when I saw that little guy's happy face suddenly get a sad expression on it and saw him drop his head, like a friendly little dog does when you scold it, I felt sorry for him and decided that maybe seventeen seconds' lost time wouldn't make any difference. So I shoved the speed control lever of the motor back to "Slow," and shoved the steering handle around so we'd cut a wide circle, and in a jiffy we were putt-putting slowly back toward the floating bottle.

You see, all the members of the Sugar Creek Gang were almost as interested in Little Jim's new hobby as he was. For about a week he'd been getting all the old empty whiskey bottles he could find. Being an honest-to-goodness Christian boy who hated whiskey because it was a terrible enemy of mankind and made so many people in the world so sad and caused so much trouble, he had been putting what is called "a gospel tract" in them and a little note which he scribbled in his own handwriting. A gospel tract, just in case you might never have heard what one is, is a little folder with a printed message on it telling whoever reads it something important out of the Bible, especially how to be saved and become a Christian. The kinda awkward scribble which Little Jim always tucked into each bottle along with the tract always said the same thing, which was: "Whoever finds this, please believe that God loves you. If you're not saved, remember Jesus died on the cross for you, and wants you to pray to Him and thank Him for doing it, and give your heart to Him *quick*. If you don't know how to do it, send me your name and address and I'll send you a free book telling you how." Then Little Jim would sign his name which was *Jim Foote,* and he also gave his Sugar Creek address.

Then he'd cork up the bottle good and tight and toss it out into the lake for somebody to find and read. We'd all been having fun helping him, and we could hardly wait till we got back home to Sugar Creek to see if Little Jim had any mail from anybody who had found one of his notes.

You see, Little Jim had his mind made up that some time maybe when he was grown-up, he was going to be a missionary, but he couldn't wait that long to be one so he was trying to be one *now.* He being that kind of a swell little guy and also being one of my best friends, I had decided I wasn't going to wait till I was any more grownup than I was, before doing it too.

In a jiffy our boat was gliding slowly up alongside the bobbing bottle, and Circus, who was closer to it than Little Jim, reached out his hand and caught hold of it and started to hand it over to Little Jim. Then he let out a yell and said, "Hey, it's got something tied to it!"

And sure enough, it had. I could see there was a piece of heavy fishing line, tied around the bottle's neck, and that something was fastened to the other end away down in the water somewhere.

3

Say, the very second I realized there was something tied to the other end of that fishing line I was afraid it might be some heavy object, and at the rate our boat was traveling, if Circus held onto the bottle, the line might break. So I yelled to him, "Hey, let go! The line might break!" At the same time, I quick shut off the gas to almost nothing and swung the boat around in a half circle, so, in case Circus *didn't* let go, the line wouldn't have too much strain on it and break. I was wondering what on earth might be on the other end.

My motor made a couple of smoky coughs right that minute and stopped, which was maybe a good thing because we *might* have broken the line, if it hadn't.

You could have knocked me over with a pine needle when we found out what kind of a message was in that bottle. There wasn't anything on the other end of the very strong fishing line except a great big old-fashioned horseshoe. It was

25

covered with weeds and lake bottom dirt, which meant it had been used as a weight so the waves wouldn't wash the bottle away.

It only took us a few jiffies to read what was in the bottle, because we didn't even have to take out the cork. A piece of paper with black printing on it was rolled up inside, with the words as plain as anything visible right through the glass. Poetry read them out loud to us in his squawky voice:

Dear Fisherman Friend: This is one of the best places on the lake for Crappie fishing. Try it here Monday through Saturday an hour before and after sundown. But on Sunday at 11:00 and 7:30, come to THE CHURCH OF THE CROSS, Bemidji, Minnesota, where we are fishing for men. We will be pleased to welcome you. Please leave this marker here for others to read. And remember that Christ Jesus came into the world to save sinners, which means "you, me and anybody else."

The Pastor

P.S. Tune in the CHURCH OF THE CROSS radio broadcast every afternoon at 4:00.

Well, our boat was maybe only a few yards from where we'd first seen the bottle floating, which, as I told you, was not far from the shore, just straight out from the old Indian cemetery. So we took the oars which every motor boat ought to have in it,

26

and rowed a few strokes back to where we thought the bottle had been floating before. Poetry was about to put it carefully back into the water when Dragonfly piped up and said, "Let's tie some *other* weight on it. I'd like to keep that horseshoe for good luck."

"You're crazy," Poetry squawked. "That'd be stealing, and stealing would mean *bad* luck."

Just that second there was a long high-pitched quavering cry of a loon from somewhere on the lake, and Dragonfly who'd been having a hard time getting used to a loon's lonely cry, looked up quick like he had heard a ghost, while at the same time Circus let the horseshoe sink into the lake. A second later, there was the bottle floating on the surface of the water again, lying flat, which meant that the horseshoe was really on the bottom and the line was loose.

Right away, I adjusted the motor for starting, gave a quick sharp pull on the starter knob and away we all went again, racing up the shore toward the Narrows where we knew the river flowed from this lake into the one our camp site was on. In another ten minutes, we'd be there and Big Jim would help us decide what to do about John Till.

It was a wonderful ride and if we hadn't been so excited, we would have enjoyed the scenery like we'd done once before when we were riding

27

through the Narrows. The Narrows were almost a half mile long, and there was a little current but the river was flowing in the same direction we were going, so in only a few minutes we were on our own lake, and the pretty black-shrouded motor was carrying us fast straight for camp.

Poetry yelled "Remember yesterday afternoon when it rained and we were in Old John's cabin, we found that little portable radio and when we turned it on, we heard a Christian program? I'll bet that was the Church of the Cross program."

Then Little Jim, who was sitting beside Dragonfly with one hand holding onto his stick and the other onto the side of the boat, piped up and said with a tickled grin on his face, "Radio's a good way to fish for men. It's like casting with a terribly long line clear out where the fish really are."

"Old John Till's a *fish*, all right," Dragonfly said, "only he drinks whiskey instead of water. I hope when we get him captured, he'll have to go to jail the rest of his life."

I noticed that Circus's monkey-looking face had a very serious expression on it for a minute, like what Dragonfly had said had been like a pin sticking him somewhere. All of a sudden I remembered that Circus's dad had once been a drunkard himself. Even while we were racing along with the oak and white birch and Balm of Gilead and pine trees whizzing past, and our boat cutting a fierce fast V through the water, I was remembering one summer night back at Sugar Creek when there had been a big tent filled with people and a big choir and an evangelist preaching. Nearly all of the members of the Sugar Creek Gang had been saved. And when Circus himself had walked down the grassy aisle to the front to confess the Saviour, all of a sudden Old Dan Browne, Circus's drinking dad, who had been outside of the tent listening, had come rushing in, running down the aisle with tears in his eyes and voice, crying out loud, "That's my boy! That's my boy!" And that very night God had saved Old Dan Browne clear through, so that he hadn't taken a drop of whiskey or beer since. From then on he was a good worker and his family had had enough to eat.

Circus must have been thinking the same thing, 'cause when Dragonfly said that about Old hook-nosed John Till's going to jail, he looked across the top of all the heads of the rest of the gang and straight into my eyes. I could see the muscles of his jaw working like he was thinking hard. I also noticed that his fists were doubled up terribly tight, and remembered that he hated whiskey worse than anything else in the world, because it had made his mother very unhappy for a long time.

Little Jim called out to all of us then and said, "What about *Tom?* What'll we tell *him?*"

"And what *will* we tell him?" I thought—that swell little red-head who was the newest member of our gang and Old Hook-nose's boy.

Not a one of us knew. But in a little while now, at the rate we were flying, we'd be back in camp where Big Jim and Little Tom Till were. And we'd have to tell them that we had Tom's dad locked up in the icehouse, and that he was probably what police called an accomplice of the actual kidnapper we'd caught last week.

I was terribly disappointed at what Big Jim decided to do as soon as we'd told him. We didn't want Tom to hear it, as he would start feeling terribly sad and have all the rest of his vacation spoiled—although of course he'd *have* to find it out sooner or later.

Big Jim heard our motor and came out to the end of the long dock where the mailbox was to meet us, wondering who on earth we were at first, coming in with a highpowered motor and a different boat. Little Tom wasn't in camp right then, but was up the shore visiting at a cabin owned by a man named Santa, who especially liked him. Tom was watching him build a utility boat in his work shop, so we had a chance to tell Big Jim the whole exciting story without Little Tom Till hearing it.

"Let's leave Tom where he is and all of us go back with a rope and tie him up," Dragonfly suggested.

"You're crazy," Circus said. "He might have a gun and might shoot us, and get away, and take all the rest of the ransom money with him."

"What ransom money?" Big Jim wanted to know, and then I remembered that Big Jim didn't know a thing about our digging in the old ice-house for the money and finding it sewed up inside a lot of fish's stomachs. So we quickly told him, and he frowned at first. Then his bright mind started to work and he just took charge of things in a jiffy.

"This is a job for the police," Big Jim told us. "You boys've done your part, and you'll get credit, but there isn't any sense in running any unnecessary risks. Let's get to a phone quick."

We all knew there wasn't any sense in trying to argue Big Jim out of that idea, and it did make good sense, although it's hard on a boy to use good sense all the time, on account of his not being used to it.

The first good sense we used was to quick carry

the money down to Santa's cabin and lock it up in his boathouse. The nearest telephone being farther on up the lake at a resort, Santa and Big Jim took Santa's boat and motored terribly fast in that direction, leaving Poetry and Circus and Little Jim and Dragonfly and Tom Till and me standing there by the boathouse to wait till they came back from phoning the police.

I looked into Poetry's bluish eyes and he into mine. We both felt pretty sad. It was going to be a *little* fun watching the police surround the icehouse though, and seeing them capture our criminal. "It'll be fun to watch him come out of that icehouse with his long hairy arms up in the air," Dragonfly said. Little Tom looked up from what he'd been doing, which was tucking the stem of an oxeye daisy through the button hole of his shirt. That little guy always likes to wear a wild flower of some kind. He asked, "Watch *who* come out of an icehouse—*what* icehouse?"

And Dragonfly, not thinking but letting the very first thought that came into his head just splash right out of his mouth, said, "Why Old hook-nosed John—"

But that was as far as his dumb sentence got, for Circus who was quicker than a cat, whirled around and clapped his hand over his mouth just in time to stop him at the word "John."

But it was too late to save Little Tom's feelings. I saw a sad look come into his bluish eyes and both fists double up quick, and I knew he was both sad and mad. He looked like he knew Dragonfly meant his dad, because he had called him "Old hook-nose John—," but the part about coming out of an icehouse with his hairy arms up in the air puzzled him. I saw him swallow hard like there was a lump in his throat, and he said, "You mean my dad's locked up somewhere? What for? What's he done?"

I'd been calling John Till "Old Hook-nose" myself when I'd been talking to the rest of the gang and when I thought about him, but somehow right that second it sort of seemed like we ought to get a more respectable, better name for him.

I knew we had to tell Tom the truth, since he heard Dragonfly say that, but I was mad at Dragonfly for a minute. I said, "Listen, you, Dragonfly Gilbert [which is his last name], you can stop calling him 'Old Hook-nose,' when you've got a nose that turns south at the end yourself!"

Then because Tom would have to know the truth some time, all of us helped each other tell him the whole story, which you already know.

While we were doing it, Tom wouldn't look us in the eye, but was picking blue flowers and tucking them into a little bouquet in his hand. Then he straightened up and looked all around in a quick circle like he was expecting to see the police coming. Also he looked out toward the lake like he was listening for the motor of Santa and Big Jim coming back.

There wasn't any motor sound though, but at that very second I heard the very sad sound of a mourning dove from up in a tree somewhere above us, saying, "*Coo, coo, coo, coo.*" Then almost the second the last "coo" was finished, there was a sort of vibrating musical sound about thirty feet above us, and I knew it was the wings of the dove as it flew away or maybe from one tree to another.

Little Jim, who had my binoculars, swished them up to his eyes and looked, just as little red-haired Tom Till said, "If my dad gets caught, he'll have to go to jail for a terribly long time, and we won't have any dad, and it'll break my mother's—"

He suddenly broke off what he was saying, got a tearful expression on his freckled face, and then because he couldn't stand to have any of us see him cry, he turned like a flash and started running back toward camp as fast as he could go, stumbling awkwardly as though he had a lot of tears in his eyes that were blinding him and he couldn't see where he was going.

4

WELL, WHEN YOU SEE one of your best friends running and stumbling along like that, and know there are tears in his eyes and that he has a great big heavy ache in his heart, you sort of get tears in your eyes yourself. All in a flash, while his red hair was bobbing down that weed-grown path toward camp, I was remembering that the first time I'd ever seen him was when he and his bad big brother Bob belonged to a gang of tough town boys that had come out in the country one afternoon and had been eating up all the strawberries that grew on Strawberry Hill. Our gang had happened onto them while they were doing it, and for some reason we'd gotten into a fierce fist fight. Tom's hard-knuckled fist had whammed me on the nose; and for a dozen fierce fist-flying minutes he and I had been enemies.

But a lot of things had happened after that. Tom and I had made up and he was now one of the best friends I had. The whole gang liked him a lot, and we didn't hold it against him that his big brother Bob was what people called a "juvenile delinquent," and his dad was a beer- and whiskey-drinking infidel that acted like he hated God and the church and was too lazy to work for a living.

So when I saw Tom go stumbling away like that, I got a big lump in my throat, and started off after him, not too fast though, 'cause I didn't think he wanted anybody to follow him.

When I got to camp, I heard Tom inside our director's tent moving around doing something. I couldn't guess what. It seemed like I was sort of spying on him, and I hated to make him feel worse by looking at his tears, if he was still crying. So I slipped into the other tent and peeped through the nearly closed flaps. And then all of a sudden I saw Tom thrust open the flap of his tent real quick and dive out and around it, and start on the run up the lake in the other direction, carrying his small old-looking brown suitcase, and I wondered, "What on earth!"

I was so surprised for a minute that I couldn't even move, and it wasn't until after Tom disappeared on the path running as fast as he could with that suitcase flopping along beside him that I realized he was probably so ashamed he was going to try to run away and go back home.

Then I came to life, dived out of my tent, and

started after him, yelling, "Hey! Tom! Wait for me. I want to tell you something."

I didn't know what I wanted to tell him, but if he would only wait till I got there I could probably think of something. I certainly didn't want him to go home.

Behind me I could hear the sound of Santa's motor on the lake, and—well, I darted after Tom Till as fast as my excited legs could carry me.

I was a little longer legged than Tom, and caught up with him after only a short run and grabbed him, and said, "You're a swell guy, Tom. The whole gang likes you."

He dropped his suitcase, pulled loose, and darted around behind the big bole of a Norway pine tree, where he stopped. I could see part of him, and could tell by the way one of his elbows was moving that he was wiping tears out of his eyes, maybe with the back of his hand.

I tried to coax him to go back to camp with me, but he wouldn't. "Everybody hates me," he sobbed. But he knew *I* really *liked* him, as I had proved it to him at different times. He slumped down in the grass and let himself sort of sob and talk at the same time, and also sniffle. He wasn't looking at me but straight ahead in the direction of a little cluster of bright yellow mustard flowers like the kind that grow along the edge

39

of our garden back at Sugar Creek if you let them. They are very pretty but are pests, and if you give them a chance they will spread in a few years all over a field or fence row.

Seeing those pretty mustard flowers and knowing that Tom was crying on account of his dad, and also on account of his mother, I thought of my own parents and how when I catch a cold, my brown-haired mom makes a mustard plaster and puts it on my chest.

"You're a swell guy," I said to Tom, and felt awful warm inside my heart toward him and wished he was my brother and that I could do something to make him happy.

Tom seemed to remember then that he had a handkerchief in his pocket. He pulled it out and blew his freckled nose and then he just sort of straightened up quick like he'd thought of something important. "Where IS the icehouse?" he asked me, and scrambled to his feet.

I wondered what he had on his mind, because his face looked like he'd made up his mind to do something terribly important which he was afraid to do but was going to do anyway. But he wouldn't tell me until I said I wouldn't show him where the icehouse was if he *didn't* tell me. So he told me. Would you believe it? This is what he said. "I want to get there before the cops do and talk to him about something. I want to *tell* him something."

I looked at his tearful eyes and his sniffling nose and his freckled face and liked him even better than ever. I thought I ought to ask Big Jim what he thought, as he had a lot of bright ideas about things like that.

Right away we found Big Jim who had just come back with Santa from phoning the police, and I was surprised when he said, "Nothing doing. It's up to the police now."

But Tom got a stubborn expression on his face and said, "I've GOT to talk to him. You've GOT to take me there, 'cause after the cops get him I won't have any chance."

We were standing down on the beach at the time. Tom's bare toes were digging themselves into the sand, and he was still sniffling a little and swallowing. "I want to ask him to give up when the police come for him," he said.

"You won't *need* to ask him *that*," Dragonfly who had come up just that second, said. "He'll *have* to give up."

"He might *not*," Tom said. "He might kill some of the police—he might even kill himself— if he's—if he's been drinking. My dad's pretty fierce when he's half drunk and mad at the same time."

41

I looked at Big Jim's face. He was looking down at the boat with the pretty black-shrouded outboard motor attached to the stern, and the muscles of his jaw were working like they do when he's thinking. Barry, our camp director, hadn't come back yet because he had to be away all night, so Big Jim was still our boss.

"Is that your dad's motor?" Big Jim asked Tom Till, pointing toward it, and Tom said, "I don't know. He always wanted one like that, but I don't think he had enough— (*sniff—sniff*) —money to buy one."

Just that second we heard a horn blowing out on the lake and knew it was the mail boat coming. The boat brought letters from our parents for most of us, and one in Little Tom Till's mother's handwriting which was addressed to him.

Tom held it in his hands, studying it. Then he opened it and read it, while different ones of us read our own letters, only I kept watching him out of the corner of my eyes. Then I saw him quick shuffle over to Big Jim and shove the letter into his hand and say, "Read *that!*"

Big Jim had been reading a letter in a very smooth, pretty handwriting in green ink. I knew it was from Sylvia, whose pop was our Sugar Creek minister and who Big Jim thought was extra nice. We all agreed. Jim tucked Sylvia's letter inside his shirt pocket and read Tom's mom's letter, and—well, that was what decided us.

"All right, Gang," Big Jim said to us in a quick authoritative voice, when he'd finished Tom's letter. "Let's get going. We've got to get this letter to John Till before the police get there. Circus, you and Dragonfly run down to the boathouse and wait with Santa. That icehouse is on some new lake-front property he bought two weeks ago, and he'll show the police how to get there."

"I want to go with you," Dragonfly whined.

"You can come with the police, if they'll let you," Big Jim said. "They'll be here as quick as they can."

And so Big Jim, Little Tom Till, Little Jim and Poetry and I got into the big boat, and I let Big Jim run the motor because he was going to, anyway. First, we checked to see if we had enough gas, and also we tossed in enough life-preserver pillows for each of us. Little Jim put on his lifesaver vest just to be still safer, and in a few jiffies we were off. Big Jim ran the boat almost as well as I could, and I only had to tell him once what to do, but he had already done it.

I won't take time to tell you much about that fast ride, but we almost flew up the lake, and through the Narrows, swishing under the bridge and into the other lake in what seemed like a few minutes.

Just after we'd swished *under* the bridge and out into that other lake the icehouse was on, Little Jim yelled, "Hey! There's a long black car just going across now. I'll bet that's the cops."

I couldn't hear the boards of the bridge or the car's motor, because our own motor was making so much noise. It felt good though to be working with the police, and it also felt good to know there were really a lot of big strong men in our country who were interested in doing what Dad calls "protecting society from wicked men." Only with Little Tom there in the boat beside me, being such a swell little guy, it seemed too bad to think of his dad as a real criminal, but he was anyway! Even while we raced up that other shore past the Indian cemetery and the whiskey bottle which I noticed was still there— the one that had the printed gospel message in it—I couldn't help but wonder if maybe nearly every criminal in the world had some relatives such as a brother or a sister or maybe a wife or a boy or girl in his family who felt like Little Tom was feeling right that minute. He looked awfully sad. For some reason it seemed that maybe it was also a big crime to hurt people's hearts like Tom's was being hurt right that second.

44

I sort of let my mind fly away like a balloon in the sky for a minute, and was thinking, "What if John Till was my dad, and I was on my way to an old icehouse where he was locked up, to give him a letter from my swell brown-haired mom? And what if in twenty minutes maybe he would be arrested for being an accomplice in a kidnapping and might not only have to go to jail for life, but might even have to have what is called 'capital punishment' done to him—which is being electrocuted or hung?"

Little Jim piped up with a question then that burst my balloon and brought me down to earth. It was, "How'll we get the letter to your dad? We don't dare open the door."

Poetry's bright mind thought of a way. He said, "We'll make a ladder out of ourselves and push Tom up, so he can poke the letter through the crack between the logs." That was a good idea.

A little later, we rounded a bend in the lake and Big Jim steered straight toward the beach in front of the old log icehouse, where we'd left John Till only a little less than an hour before. My heart was pounding fast and hard. I was feeling tense inside on account of Tom, wondering what was in the letter and also what Tom wanted to tell his pop.

Big Jim shut off the motor at just the right

speed, and we glided up to the shore. After beaching the boat, and tossing the anchor onto the shore, we scrambled out, and right away were sneaking up close to the icehouse.

We moved quietly so we wouldn't be heard, although John Till could have heard our motor when we were coming in, I supposed.

"Sh!" Big Jim said to us, he and Tom leading the way as we crept up closer. I didn't know what would happen next, but in a jiffy I found out, 'cause Big Jim stopped the rest of us and sent Tom on toward the icehouse alone. I peered through the leaves of some wild chokecherry shrubs we were crouching behind. Then I heard Tom's pathetic voice that had a kind of a quaver in it like he was scared, calling out, "DAD."

We listened to see if there was any answer, but couldn't hear any. Then Tom's voice called again, a little louder, real close to the side of the old log house. I had both hands up to my ears, but there wasn't a sound, except right that second I heard a very-pretty wren's song that sounded half like a fast mixed-up whistling tune and half like the spring water that trickles out of the rocks not far from the old swimming hole back at Sugar Creek.

Then Tom called still louder, *"DAD!* It's ME —TOM! *I've got a letter for you from Mother!"*

But say, that icehouse was as quiet as if it had

been an extra large gravehouse in an Indian cemetery.

Tom turned around then and looked in our direction with a question mark on his face.

All of us came out into the open and went toward him, not knowing what to think. In a little while the police would be there, and it'd be too late for Tom to tell his dad what he wanted to tell him or to give him the letter or anything. Right that very second, I heard a fast motor coming on the lake somewhere and wondered if it might be Santa's big boat, bringing the police and Circus and Dragonfly.

Poetry, who had been with me the night before in the middle of the night, when we'd seen John Till wide awake, taking a string of fish down to the lake from his cottage, whispered to us and said, "Maybe he was so tired he went to sleep. Let's all go up and surround the icehouse and yell him awake." We decided that might be a good idea, and right away we hurried toward where Tom Till was. Poetry and I hurried around to the side where the door was.

You could have knocked me over with a puff of wind. There in front of my astonished eyes was that old great big icehouse door, wide open, on its rusty hinges. *Our prisoner had escaped!*

5

WELL, THAT WAS THAT and it was terribly disappointing. Poetry and I stood staring at that open door, wondering what had happened. Who had opened it and let John Till out and where had he gone? Was he hiding somewhere close by, and might he spring from behind something any minute and knock the living daylights out of one of us?

Big Jim and the rest of the gang came running around right away to where we were, and as soon as we found that our prisoner was *really* gone, we looked at each other with sad and disappointed eyes.

I looked at Tom who had his mom's letter in his hands, and noticed it was all crinkled, like letters get when you squish them up tight in your hands.

"What'll we do?" different ones of us asked the rest of us, and waited for Big Jim to decide what. He looked at Tom, who looked sad and surprised and disappointed. For a second it seemed like

49

he didn't belong to our gang at all but was a strange boy—like a little lost duckling that gets hatched out with a nestful of fluffy little chickens in our chicken yard and follows the mother hen around with the chickens but doesn't do what they do or look like they look.

"We've got to find my dad!" Tom said, and stooped down and picked a small white five-petalled flower which I noticed was growing beside the icehouse on a little plant about five or six inches high. The flower plant had shining green three-sectioned leaves with little notches in them. Little Jim saw him pick it and stooped down quick and picked one himself, and said, "It's a goldthread flower. *Goody!*" which goes to show that even in an exciting time that little guy can be interested in something else. I remembered that he had a flower guide book, and besides having a hobby of putting a gospel message in whiskey bottles, he was also trying, while we were on our vacation, to find as many wild flowers as he could. He wrote their names in a notebook to show to our teacher that fall when school started at Sugar Creek.

Tom seemed to be thinking. He didn't answer Big Jim at all, but looked down at his goldthread and at the crinkled up letter in his hand, and then began to try to push the goldthread stem

50

through the button in his shirt beside the oxeye daisy that was still there.

I won't have room right at this part of the story to tell you what happened when the police came, which they did pretty quick, except to say that as soon as they believed that we hadn't let John Till out ourselves, they dug around in the icehouse and found a lot of other fish with part of the ransom money in them—enough, when they added up what *we* had locked up in Santa's boathouse, to make over $20,000.

But where was the rest of the money? Nobody knew, and nobody knew where John Till had disappeared to. He wasn't in the old cabin which we found out he'd rented from Santa. It was the same cabin we'd seen him in once, and which you know about if you've read the story, *The Sugar Creek Gang Digs for Treasure*. Both the cabin and the icehouse belonged to Santa who had bought them from a real-estate man only a few weeks before.

It was awful hard on Tom to know that even though his dad was free, the police were still after him, and nobody knew when he'd be caught, or whether he'd try to resist arrest and be shot and maybe killed.

Another thing that made it hard for Tom was the letter from his mother which he let me see, and when I read it I couldn't blame Tom for feeling sad. Part of it said, "I think maybe your father is up in the North Woods somewhere where you boys are camping, Tom. I don't know for sure, but we got a notice from the bank that the interest on our loan is past due, and it *has* to be paid. If he stops in to visit you, please give him this letter. As you know, I gave him the egg money I'd saved up all winter and summer, and he was going to take it to the bank just before he left. I'm sure he went fishing, because his tackle is gone. But don't worry, Tommy boy, we'll make out somehow. The Lord is on our side. You just keep on having good boyish fun and learning all you can in the evening campfire Bible lessons. You and I will keep on praying for your dad and your brother Bob, that some day they'll both be saved. Our minister called this morning, and he's praying too. And he says God can do things nobody thinks He can. . . ."

There was more in Tom's letter from home. Tom's white rabbit had carrots for breakfast and seemed quite content but was probably lonesome for Tom, and the new potatoes in the garden would make awful good raw-fried potatoes for supper when Tom came home. . . . It really was a swell letter, the same kind I got from my mom, with scribbling all around the edges, things for a boy to remember not to do and why. Don't catch cold, and be careful not to fall out of the boats—things like that which always worry a mother, who can't help it because she is a mother.

We kept on the lookout for John Till every minute of that day and the next when we took a trip to the headwaters of the Mississippi. Little Jim took notes on that trip so he could show them to our teacher that fall when we got back to Sugar Creek, and one of his notes was:

"The Mississippi river is 2406 miles long from the place where it starts at Itasca Lake, Minnesota, to where it stops at the Gulf of Mexico."

We started out early in the morning in our station wagon for Itasca State Park, where there was a great big blue-watered lake that is 8 miles in circumference. There, in a pretty shady park, we parked and all of us scrambled out and swished along following each other in a little winding path till we came to the lake. There was a small stream of water about twelve feet across and about a foot or less deep flowing out of it, making a very pretty noise which sounded like it was half a sigh and half a ripple. The sound was also mixed up with the voices of different birds which were singing all around and above us in the bushes and trees.

We all were quiet for awhile, not seeing what we had expected to see when we saw the source of the Mississippi, but it was very interesting anyway.

Little Jim got a mischievous twinkle in his eyes, and then he quick stooped down and in a jiffy had both his shoes and socks off. I knew he was going to wade across the stream which was shallow and narrow. Right away we all had our shoes and socks off and every single one of us waded clear across the Mississippi river.

"Here we are," I said to us, as most of us stopped out in the middle of the Mississippi river and gathered ourselves into a half-circle with our faces looking toward one of the shores where our camp director had a camera waiting to take our picture.

Standing there, squinting my eyes in the direction of the camera and also in the direction of the sun, I happened to remember a brand new Paul Bunyan story which Poetry had made up once and which you maybe know about if you've read *The Sugar Creek Gang Goes North.* Old Babe, which is Paul Bunyan's blue ox, was swimming in the headwaters of the Mississippi river and the blue began to come off and make the water blue; and because the Mississippi flows through a lot of the lakes in Minnesota, pretty soon all the lakes became what are called "blue-watered lakes."

Of course it was only a legend. Paul Bunyan, as you know, was a legendary lumberman who was extra large; and Babe, the blue ox, was his best friend and went everywhere he went, just like a boy's dog follows a boy around.

Anyway, while we were having our picture taken, I remembered the story Poetry told about how the lakes got their blue water. So I looked down quick at Poetry's large feet and at all the seventy different-shaped and different-lengthed toes on the fourteen feet of all seven of us. I tried to think of something funny to say, but it really wasn't as funny as I thought it would be. "If all the fish in the lakes up here get terribly sick and die before long, it'll be because the barrel-shaped boy in our gang didn't wash his feet before he waded across the Mississippi river."

And that's how it happened that I wished I had brought along a change of clothes, because for some reason what I said made Poetry peeved. He quick shoved his shoulder against me, and because I was standing in fast-flowing water half-way up to my knees anyway, when I stepped side-ways to try to get my balance I stepped on a slippery rock in the river bed, lost my whole balance and the next thing I knew I was sitting down on the bottom of the Mississippi river, the water coming clear up to my stomach.

Right away Barry pointed his camera in our direction and took another picture.

That reminded Poetry of a riddle which he quick asked. It was: "Say, gang, what is it that stays in bed all day, spends all its time at the bank and never stops running?"

"A *river*," Dragonfly said and sneezed twice because he is not only allergic to different pollens but to sudden changes of temperature—the water in that little narrow babbling stream being almost cold.

Well, that was all that happened on that trip, except one thing. It was that one thing that helped make our next adventure, which was a fishing trip for walleyes, extraordinarily interesting and exciting.

Not having brought along any extra clothes, I had to walk in my wet trousers back to our station wagon, which wasn't any too much fun for me. There they made me undress and lie down where I wouldn't be seen while some of the gang wrung the water out of my trousers and also out of the tail of my shirt. I would have to wait till they dried enough for me to put them on, which meant I had to let the rest of the gang visit a very special curio shop without me, while my clothes were hanging on a limb in the sun. Poetry who was about my best friend was already sorry I was all wet, and we made up as soon as I found out he was going to stay with me to keep me company.

I gave Little Jim some money out of my billfold and told him to pick out something he especially thought my little sister, Charlotte Ann, would like. I knew that in a few days we were all going to break camp and drive back to Sugar Creek, and I wanted to take home a few things made by the Indians.

Poetry and I were alone awhile, with me lying under a blanket on the back seat of the station wagon. We talked over all the wonderful experiences of our vacation, and decided it had been the best camping trip we'd had in our lives.

"Only one thing would make it the best we ever could have," he said, and when I said, "What?" he didn't answer for a minute. He was sitting in the open door not far from me and I was lying on my back, wishing the hot sun and the breeze would hurry up and get my clothes a little drier so I could put them on. He had his back to me and I couldn't see his fat face, but his squawky voice had a sort of a faraway sound in it like he was thinking of something extra serious.

When he still didn't answer me, I asked him again and he said quietly, "I feel sorry for Tom." Then his voice sort of choked and I guessed that he liked that little red-haired guy just as well as I did. Right that second if anybody had asked me anything, I wouldn't have answered either, 'cause I felt my eyes stinging, and there would have been a tear in my voice, and boys don't like to have anybody see tears in their eyes or hear them in their voices.

Pretty soon though, Poetry spoke again with his back still toward me, "Did you ever read this verse in the Bible?"

If I hadn't been already down, you could have knocked me over with a fish scale when I realized what he was doing. Say, he had taken his little leather New Testament out of his shirt pocket and, looking through it, had found a verse he thought was extra good.

As you maybe know, an official part of the equipment of anybody who belongs to the Sugar Creek Gang, is a small pocket New Testament. We carry one with us nearly all the time, and every one of us not only reads it every day but we aren't ashamed to let anybody know we do it either. But on account of being boys and feeling like nearly all boys do, we didn't talk about the Bible very much except in camp-fire meetings or at Sunday school, and only once in a while when two or three of us were together. Little Jim and I did more of it than any of the rest of us. That's because he—well, he had a keen little mind and thought more about it, I guess, and was always getting such good ideas. Also Little Jim was glad he was alive. Not a boy in the world *would* be alive if God hadn't made him, and also if God didn't *keep* him alive. And there isn't a boy in the world that's dumb enough to want to be dead, which is why a boy ought to be glad to love God and to be kind to Him. Little Jim always was.

Anyway, when Poetry asked me if I had ever read "this verse," I said, "What verse?" So he read it to me, with his back still turned. It was out of the book of Matthew, chapter 18, and was the nineteenth verse. It said, *"If two of you shall agree on earth as touching any thing that they shall ask, it shall be done for them of my Father which is in heaven."*

It made me feel good inside to even think about the Bible, especially since I knew both of us believed what we were talking about. I just lay there, looking through the station wagon window up at the pretty branches of a pine tree that grew not very far away. I was also listening to the gurgling of the water close by and felt something kinda warm in my heart, like Poetry and God and I had a secret of some kind. When we finished telling each other what we thought the verse meant, we had made up our minds that we were going to stick together until Little Tom's dad was saved.

"Let's shake on it," Poetry said, and swung around, and shoved his fat hand in my direction. I grabbed it quick, and said, "Shake."

"Shake," he said again, then we prayed together for Tom's dad, and I felt good inside.

I noticed the branches of the pine tree above me were swaying in the wind, and I knew my clothes were drying pretty fast—I hoped.

A little later we heard the gang coming. I knew it was the gang because it sounded like a flock of blackbirds gathering in the woods in a Sugar Creek autumn getting ready for migrating to a warmer country. It also sounded like a flock of crows with a few scolding blue jays mixed in with them and maybe a harsh-voiced shrieking kingfisher joining in. Dragonfly was the rattling-voiced kingfisher, and Circus, the scolding blue jay.

My clothes were dry enough for me to put them on if, while we drove along, I'd sit on the leather seat of the station wagon, which I did. Away we went, back to camp and to the next day's fishing trip.

"Look what I got for Charlotte Ann," Little

Jim said to me, and shoved over to me a couple of small rubber balloons. "They cost only ten cents apiece," he said proudly, and handed me my change.

I was a little disappointed, but didn't want to say so, 'cause Little Jim had such a happy grin on his face to think he had saved me money. And I was also sure Charlotte Ann would be tickled to see the balloons blown up nice and big. Most babies laugh and reach out their hands for them the very minute they see them.

I tucked the two balloons in my shirt pocket beside my New Testament and buttoned the flap, and forgot about them, until the next day when we were on a very special fishing trip for wall-eyed pike.

Boy oh boy, it was going to be a wonderful trip, I thought, and we were going to fish, not for small fish like blue gills and crappies, which people call "pan" fish, but for big walleyes, to pack and ship home to our folks at Sugar Creek. Also, we were going to keep our eyes open every second to see if we could find any trace of John Till.

6

I WAS CERTAINLY GLAD our little Indian friend, Snow-in-the-face, was well enough to be our guide on our fishing trip for walleyed pike. As you maybe know, he'd been very sick but almost right away after our gang had called to see him, which we did the very next day after we had come up north, he had started to get better. And now, today, he was coming to our camp to visit us and to guide us to the best fishing waters for walleyed pike, so we could all catch our "limit," which is eight walleyes apiece. Multiplying eight fish by seven boys, which any teacher will tell you you can't do, we'd have fifty-six fish to pack in ice and ship back to Sugar Creek for our parents to see and to help us eat. Boy oh boy, it was going to be fun!

About three o'clock that afternoon, after the gang had all had a rest hour, little Snow-in-the-face and his big Indian brother, Eagle Eye, came putt-putting in a canoe, straight to our shore.

There was a lot of excitement around camp for a while, while all of us finished getting our equipment ready. Our two big fishing boats were equipped with life-preserver pillows, which nobody ought to go on a fishing trip without.

It had been a terribly hot day and the sun up in the sky poured its yellowish heat down on us something fierce as our boats plowed their wet way out across the waves toward an island. It also reflected back up into our faces from the water and made me glad I had on a pair of dark glasses to protect my eyes from the extra bright light.

Snow-in-the-face was in the boat I was in, along with Little Jim, Poetry and Dragonfly, and we were following the other boat which had Eagle Eye and Big Jim and Circus and Little Tom Till. Barry had stayed home to write letters and to look after camp.

In a little while our boats neared the pretty pine- and spruce-covered island, circled around it to the other side where we anchored in a little cove, not more than thirty yards from each other, in some quiet water.

That swell little reddish-brown-faced Indian boy with his bright black eyes and straight black hair didn't even use a pole, but had a big heavy line which he dropped down over the side of our boat. I was sitting beside him in the middle seat, with Poetry sitting in the stern close to the outboard motor. Dragonfly was in the prow. Little Jim was in front of me in a seat by himself, with his life vest on, which meant he was even safer than the rest of us, because if our boat had upset or we had fallen out, he would have been ready to float to shore without having to hold onto a pillow.

In only a few jiffies we all had our hooks baited with live chubs and were waiting for somebody— either in our boat or in the other one—to catch the first fish. The very second one of us would get a walleye, we'd know we'd found a school of them, and in a little while we'd all get bites and catch fish at the same time, on account of walleyes stick together like a gang of boys.

"Eagle Eye found this place last year," Snow-in-the-face said. "Fish bite here when they don't any place else on the lake."

But say, after we all had sat there and waited and waited and pulled our lines in and out of the water for an hour and not a one of us had caught a single fish, or even had a nibble, it looked as if having a good guide wasn't any good.

Snow-in-the-face had a pucker on his brown forehead and looked worried.

"Ho hum," I thought, and shifted myself to another uncomfortable position on the hot boat seat I was on. Any position is uncomfortable when the fish don't bite and the deer flies are swarming around your legs and hands and biting fiercely just like you wish the fish would.

Pretty soon, I looked over at the pretty pine-covered island and wished I could go over there and sit down in the shade for awhile. I was also remembering that that was the very island I'd wanted to explore when I'd first gotten the idea of playing Robinson Crusoe and Treasure Island. My idea had got us tangled up in the mystery of the buried treasure, most of which we'd finally found. The rest of it Old John Till probably had somewhere, wherever he was, which nobody knew.

"I'm terribly hot," I said to the rest of us in our boat. "Let's go over to that island and lie down in the shade awhile." The rest of us thought it was a good idea, and so we pulled in our lazy lines and also pulled anchor and rowed over. In a little while, Poetry and I were strolling along following the shore around to the side where we could look across and see our camp away out across the lake. It was one of the prettiest islands I'd ever seen. It had great big Norway pines and spruce and Tamarack and also ferns and all kinds of wild flowers such as red-flowered wild columbine and white goldthread. In a boggy place were some pitcher plants, which had queer-looking green leaves that looked like one of the green pitchers Mom has on our sideboard at home. The leaves looked like the lips of a French horn that one of the men at Sugar Creek plays in the band on Saturday night.

We'd left Snow-in-the-face and Little Jim and Dragonfly back at the shore in the boat, 'cause Snow-in-the-face had acted like he didn't want to come with us, and Dragonfly had been so lazy and also afraid of smelling wild flowers and having to sneeze a lot. That was one of the reasons he'd come on this vacation with us, so he could get away from Sugar Creek flowers and timothy hay and ragweed and everything else which would make him sneeze.

"You know what?" Poetry said to me all of a sudden, and when I said, "No, what?" he said, "This would be a good island for John Till to hide on. Maybe when he got out of the icehouse, he came over here."

"But how could he get here? We had his boat."

"He might swim," Poetry said, but it wasn't a good idea because it was pretty far from any other shore over here, so I said, "Of course, he could rent a boat from almost any resort up here."

We were standing right that minute close to a sandy beach and the waves were washing up in a very lazy friendly way, when all of a sudden, Poetry said, "Hey, look, somebody's been here.

Somebody's had a boat beached here on the sand."
Somebody had, but it was gone now.

"Boy oh boy!" I said, all of a sudden getting excited, "and here are shoe tracks, going back into the island somewhere."

We decided to follow the tracks, which we did, but didn't find anything interesting. There might be a broken twig trail, though, like the one we'd followed before, and which you know about, may-be, but we couldn't find a thing, so we gave up and went back to Dragonfly and Snow-in-the-face and Little Jim.

"Where were you guys?" Dragonfly wanted to know, and I said, "Oh, looking for buried treas-ure."

Little Snow-in-the-face got a queer far-away ex-pression on his face, squinted his eyes and said, "Sometimes we see lights out here at night."

And then it was Dragonfly's turn to get a queer far-away expression on his face, which made it seem like he wished he was as far away as his thoughts.

Well, we decided to try fishing some more like the rest of the guys in the other boat were, but they still hadn't caught anything. We rowed out to another place and baited our hooks and tried again.

Another hour passed during which we pulled anchor and tried a half dozen different locations and still not a one of us caught a single fish and we were terribly discouraged.

"You *can* have one if you *want* one," Little Jim said.

"How?" I said, and he said, "One of those balloons I bought for you yesterday is a *rubber* fish. You can blow *it* up—maybe it's a walleye."

Well, I still had those two rubber balloons in my shirt pocket, so because I was terribly bored and didn't know what else to do, I pulled out the one that looked like it would be shaped like a fish when it was blown up. And, like the old wolf that ate up the little pigs, I huffed and I puffed and I blew the balloon up into a nice great big long fish that looked like a walleyed pike. For awhile I had something to keep my mind off being bored, because if there is anything that is harder to do than anything else, it is to sit on the seat of a boat on a hot day when the fish won't bite.

"If we get *one,* we'll get *twenty,*" Poetry said. "Walleyes go in schools, you know."

"Yeah," Little Jim piped up and said, "but fish maybe don't *have* school in *August,*" which reminded me that right after August came September, and generally in the first week of September, the Sugar Creek School started and—

I let out a fierce long sigh when I thought of

that, not because I didn't need an education but I hated to have to sit down to get one, which is what you have to do in school most of the time. The boat seat was getting harder and harder every minute.

The yellowish rubber fish I'd just blown up looked cute though, and was as fat as a butterball. For a while I let it float on the water clear out to the end of the fishing line I had tied it on. "Here, Poetry," I said to the fish, "get out there and float. You're so fat you *can't* sink," which made the real Poetry in the boat with us pretend to be peeved, and he said to me, "Oh, you go jump in the lake!"

And then—all of an excited sudden—Poetry got a big strike. He waited until he was sure it was time to set the hook, which he did at exactly the right time and in a jiffy he landed a very excited walleye; only it wasn't much bigger than a big yellow perch—hardly big enough to keep.

"O.K., Bill—hand me the stringer," he ordered me, panting with happiness. Talk about a proud grin on a boy's face. Poetry really had one.

"*What* stringer?" I said, and looked all around on the bottom of the boat for one. And—would you believe it? Not a one of us had brought along a fish stringer! The other boat was too far away for them to throw one into our boat, so Poetry just sat there with his fish in his fat hand, wondering what to do with it.

"It's too little to keep," Little Jim said. "Let him go back to his mama."

"I wish I knew where his mama is hiding," Dragonfly said. "I'd like to catch her."

"Let him go and he'll *find* his mama," Snow-in-the-face said, and had the cutest grin on his small-ish face, and that tickled me all over 'cause I could see he was as mischievous as any white-faced boy.

"It's probably a little lost child-fish," Little Jim said. "We aren't going to catch any more anyway. Let's let him go home to his parents."

Well, as you know, I had the end of my fish balloon tied air-tight shut, with a piece of old fishing line I'd had in my pocket, and it was still in the water on the opposite side of the boat. It was really cute, that little yellowish rubber fish bobbing along out there on the surface of the water.

And then Poetry yelled across to the other boat, saying, "HEY, YOU GUYS, OVER THERE! WE GOT A FISH BUT DON'T HAVE ANY STRINGER TO PUT HIM ON. WHAT'LL WE DO WITH HIM?"

Circus, being mischievous and having lots of bright ideas anyway, yelled back to us, "IF YOU'LL PUT HIM BACK IN THE WATER

AND TELL HIM TO SWIM OVER HERE, WE'LL PUT HIM ON *OUR* STRINGER!"

And that was what gave Poetry another idea which wasn't so dumb and which turned our discouraged fishing trip into a real one that was wonderful. Poetry yelled back to Circus, "SWELL IDEA, WE'LL SEND HIM OVER RIGHT AWAY!" Then he got a command in his voice and said to me, "Here, Bill, give me that line," and reached out and took it before I could make up my mind not to let him have it.

"What crazy thing are you going to do?" Dragon-fly asked, when Poetry held the fish between his knees a minute while with his two fat hands he made a double slip-knot around the walleye's tail. And then almost before anybody could have stopped him if he had wanted to, Poetry released that frisky little walleye into the water sort of like my mother does when she carefully holds an old setting hen and eases her into a coop where there is a nestful of eggs for her to sit on. Poetry said to the fish, as he let go, "Here, Wally, my friend, you go swimming straight for the other boat away over there!"

Boy, that fish certainly had lots of pep. Being out of the water for that short time hadn't hurt him a bit, although if you are going to let a fish go free after catching him, you are supposed to be very careful to handle him with wet hands, and release him under the water rather than throw him back, and he'll be more likely to live.

Say, that frisky little walleye made a fierce fast dive straight down into the water, and in a few fast seconds, the yellowish rubber balloon was bobbing up and down like it was a boy's bobber on a fishing line. And—would you believe it? It started to move right in the direction of that other boat—kinda slow though, but actually toward it.

Poetry sighed proudly, leaned back, stuck his thumbs in his arm pits and said, "See there, fish understand my language." That made Dragonfly say, "That's 'cause you talk like a fish," which, for Dragonfly, was almost a bright remark.

I could see, though, that the balloon fish was changing its course. It began working its way a little toward the left and out toward deeper water and farther from shore. We all watched it, having fun, and Poetry kept yelling to it to turn to the right and to hurry up. But pretty soon when it was maybe fifty yards from us it stopped going in one direction and began to move slowly around in a small circle.

"I'll bet he's caught on a snag," Little Snow-in-the-face said in his cute Indian voice, and it seemed like he might be right, because, even though the balloon bobbed around a little, it didn't move any farther away, but just seemed to stay more or less in the same place.

Well, we fished on, all of us hoping for another fish, but not a one of us caught one, so pretty soon we got discouraged again and pulled up anchor. Then Poetry said, "Why don't we go get him then go home, and everybody go swimming?" It sounded like a good idea. It'd be a lot more fun to do that than to sit on a hard boat seat watching a rubber balloon bobbing on the surface of a lake that didn't have any hungry fish in it.

"Let's *troll* over," Snow-in-the-face said. "Sometimes when you can't catch fish any other way, they'll bite when you do that."

Dragonfly said it was a good idea too, 'cause there might be a "lost, strayed or stolen" fish all by itself between here and that balloon. So we all left our lines in the water while Snow-in-the-face and Little Jim took the oars and rowed us kinda splashily out toward that nice yellowish balloon which I was going to get and take home to Charlotte Ann.

In a little while we were almost there, and I was getting ready to reach out my hand and get the balloon when quick as a flash I saw Little Jim's line go taut, and his pole bent down clear to the water, while he dropped his oar and quick grabbed his pole and yelled excitedly, "Hey, I've got a fish!" Just then Dragonfly's line did the same thing, and then WHAM! My own line went tight and the next thing we knew most of us in our boat found ourselves in the middle of one of the most exciting fishing experiences of our whole lives. We yelled and pulled, and our lines went singing out as our reels unwound; and almost at the same time, Dragonfly and Little Jim and Poetry and I all landed a walleye apiece, and laid them, flopping and splashing water in every direction, in the bottom of the boat.

"WE'VE STRUCK A SCHOOL!" Poetry cried. "MY FISH TOOK US RIGHT TO THEM! HE KNEW EXACTLY WHERE THEY WERE!"

7

Well you aren't supposed to yell like a lot of wild Indians on a warpath when you start catching a lot of fish, because you might scare the fish away; so almost right away we all shushed each other, and only made a noise when we caught a fish, which was just about as fast as we could bait our hooks and get our lines into the water again.

We quick anchored right close to where the balloon was, and the other boatful of the rest of the gang came rowing over as quietly as they could, and anchored close by.

Talk about excitement. We'd never had so much fishing fun in our whole lives as we were having right that minute. And then, just like Sugar Creek school getting out and the kids tumbling out the door and all going away from the red brick schoolhouse, our school of walleyes moved on and we stopped getting bites. I knew something was going to happen the minute I saw the yellowish balloon start moving fast out toward deeper water.

"Hey, look!" Dragonfly, who saw it first, said. "Wally acts like he's scared. Look at him go!"

We looked, and sure enough the balloon was bobbing up and down, and even diving clear under. Then it plunked clear under for a *long* jiffy before bouncing back up and shooting almost a foot into the air, then landed with a kersmack on the water again.

Nobody had had any bites for awhile before that, but we had enough fish for one day, and so Big Jim said, "Let's go back to camp and get supper," which was a good idea. We would come back tomorrow.

"What'll we do with Wally?" Poetry said.

"He's been a swell friend," Dragonfly said. "He ought to have some kind of appreciation."

Then Little Jim piped up good and loud and said, "Let's give him his liberty!"

Well, we had enough larger fish, and Wally really deserved some kind of a reward for helping us catch so many fish to take home to Sugar Creek. So we pulled anchor and rowed out toward where Wally was making the balloon fish bob around in such a lively style. As soon as the boat had eased alongside, I, who was closest to it, reached down my hand, caught hold of the balloon, and started to haul Wally in toward the boat. But right away my line went tight like it was fastened onto a log or snag down on the bottom of the lake. I gave a tug, but not too hard 'cause I didn't want the line to scale off any scales from Wally's tail. It is as hard on a fish to lose some of its scales as on a barefoot boy to stump his toe and knock the skin off.

"He's tangled up on something," I said, and gave another small pull and then—WHAM! There was a fierce wild lunge down there somewhere, and I felt a scared feeling racing up and down my spine. I knew Wally didn't have *that* much strength. Say, it felt as big as an excited pig running in our barnyard back at Sugar Creek—or a dog or something.

I had hold of the line as well as the balloon, and the line was cutting into my hands. I couldn't think straight, but didn't dare let loose.

Snow-in-the-face, for the very first time, got excited and yelled something to Eagle Eye in the Indian language, and then to us in English, which was, "SOME GREAT BIG FISH HAS SWALLOWED HIM."

I held on, in spite of the line's hurting my hand a little, and then, out there about ten feet, something with a big long ugly snout and with fierce eyes shot up through the waves and almost two feet in the air, and dive-splashed back in again.

There was a fierce, mad boiling of the surface

like a bomb had exploded down there in the water somewhere. I was trembling inside like any fisherman trembles when a fierce fast-fighting fish gets away after it's been hooked—only this one hadn't been hooked with a real hook. He had probably come swimming along down there under the water, looking for an early supper, like a robin hops around on our lawn at Sugar Creek looking for night crawlers, and, seeing Wally swimming lazily around, had decided to eat him.

He had probably slowly nosed his fierce ugly long snout up to Wally, and then all of a sudden made a savage rush at him with his mouth open, and had swallowed him whole, and started to swim away with him. That had scared all the other fish, which was why we'd all stopped getting bites at the same time.

Anyway, right after that fierce old fighting fish lunged up out of the water and down in again, he made a dive straight for our boat, shot under it, and pulled so hard that I had to hold on for dear life. If I'd had a long line on a fishing rod with a reel on it, I could have let the reel spin, and like fishermen do when they have a wild walleye or an enormous northern pike on their lines, I could have "played" him until he was tired out, then hauled him in. But with my line only a dozen or more feet long, I was pretty sure I didn't have a chance in the world to land him, and the next thing I knew I found out I was right. In a second it seemed, after he dived under our boat, I felt my line go sickeningly slack, and I knew I'd lost him. I couldn't tell though whether he'd broken my line, or whether he'd swallowed backwards and Wally was free again.

While the gang was groaning with disappointment, 'cause they'd seen what had happened, and while I was pulling in the lifeless line to see what was on the other end, I had a sickish feeling in the pit of my stomach like a fisherman gets when he loses a big fish.

In another jiffy I was holding up the end of the line for us to look at. Dragonfly, seeing it, said, "Poetry's slip-knot slipped."

We would have been a terribly sad gang if we hadn't already caught a lot of middle-sized walleyes.

Circus called to us from the other boat and said, "We could have put a lot of kidnapper's ransom money in a fish that big, if we'd caught him."

"There wouldn't have been much room left with Wally already inside of him," Poetry said.

For some reason I was looking at Little Jim when Poetry said that and I noticed a sad expression come on his smallish mouse-like face, and I thought it looked like he had a couple of tears in his eyes.

It had been a wonderful fishing trip and we couldn't afford to cry over a lost northern pike, which is what we all decided the big fish was. So after the other boat had pulled anchor, we started our motors, steered around the island and toward camp, with our caught fish lying in the bottom of the boat.

Little Jim was sitting in the seat in front of me, facing me as we roared along with Poetry running the motor. Different ones of us were talking and yelling to each other about all the different things that had happened—all except Little Jim who, I noticed, was extra quiet and his eyes still had that saddish look in them.

Pretty soon I leaned over and half whispered to him, "What's the matter?" He swallowed, then said, "Nothing."

"There is too," I said, just as he turned his head and gave it a quick shake. When he looked back in my direction the tears that'd been in his eyes a second before, were gone. That is the way Little Jim gets tears out of his eyes—he just turns his head away, jerks it real quick, and that shakes the tears out.

Dragonfly, who knew Little Jim had that cute little way of getting tears out without using a handkerchief, so nobody would know he had had tears in the first place, saw Little Jim do that and said to him from behind me, "Don't you know tears are salty? Fresh water fish that live in lakes don't *like* salt water."

"That's *not* funny," I said to Dragonfly over my shoulder, and was mad at him for not having more respect for Little Jim's hurt heart. I knew Little Jim's heart was hurt, when he said to me, "That wasn't much of a reward for Wally, after all he did for us."

Then just like it sometimes happens to my mother back at Sugar Creek, when she says something that has a sad thought mixed up with it, Little Jim's eyes got a couple of *new* tears in them, which he quick shook out into the lake. And then he said, as he reached his smallish cute hands toward me, "Let me hold the balloon fish for a while."

I pushed the yellowish rubber balloon toward him, and the way he took it, made me think of the way my little two-year-old baby sister, Charlotte Ann, would reach out her chubby little hands for it when I got home and showed it to her.

For a minute, while our two boats plowed along through the water, which, with the sunlight shining on the moving waves, looked like a great big lakeful of live silver, my thoughts took a hop, skip and a jump across the lake to the shore, leaped over the Chippewa forest, and high up over a lot of other lakes, like I was Paul Bunyan himself. And all of a sudden I landed right inside our kitchen at Sugar Creek, where I knew I'd be in just a few days. In my mind's eye, I saw Mom standing by our kitchen stove near the east window which has a green ivy vine trailing across the top of the outside of it. I could smell the aroma of raw-fried potatoes frying, and see the steam puffing up from the hooked spout of our kinda oldish teakettle. If, when I came in, I accidently carried in a little mud on my shoes or bare feet, Mom would say like she nearly always does, "Would you like to get the broom, Bill, and sweep out that mud which, a little while ago, came walking in on two feet?" I would know whose two feet she meant, and grin, and right away I'd step to the place where we keep our broom, which is behind the kitchen door. I wouldn't any more than get started with the dust pan and broom when Mom would say, "Be careful not to sweep *hard*, or we'll have dust in our fried potatoes."

While I was doing that, all of a sudden, I'd get tangled up and, turning around, I'd see my swell little sister Charlotte Ann, with her tiny toy broom, sweeping it around awkwardly like girls do when they're just learning how to sweep. Now

84

that she's learned to walk, she tries to do everything any of the rest of us do. She follows Mom around sweeping when Mom does, washing her hands when Mom does, and when my grayish-brown-haired mom or my reddish-brown-mustached dad sits down to read a book or a magazine she actually gets a book or a magazine and tries to read, nearly always getting the magazine upside down when she does it. In fact, she wants to do everything we do while we are doing it. Sometimes when Mom is getting supper and Charlotte Ann can't see high enough to see what Mom is doing, she gets cross and whines and fusses and pulls at Mom's dress or apron and makes a nuisance out of herself, only she doesn't know she's a nuisance. Maybe she thinks Mom is making a nuisance of *herself,* instead, for not letting her help get supper.

Yes sir, I was getting homesick for my folks, and could hardly wait till I got home next week to tell all the exciting adventures we'd had. Also, it'd be fun to watch the mail every day to see if maybe Little Jim would get any letters from anybody who would find his gospel messages which he'd been tossing out into the lake in whiskey bottles.

Thinking that, I remembered John Till and wondered where he was and what he was doing.

And all of a sudden I remembered what Poetry and I had been thinking and talking about in the station wagon when we'd been at the source of the Mississippi river, and he had found a Bible verse which said if any two of the Lord's disciples were agreed about something they wanted to pray for, they could pray for it, and the heavenly Father would do it.

Thinking that, I turned around to Poetry who, as you know, was running the motor, and looked at him, and he looked at me. I pointed to my shirt pocket, which had its flap buttoned to keep my New Testament from falling out. His eyes looked where my finger was pointing, and the expression on his mischievous happy-looking face changed to a very sober one. He kinda squinted his eyes like a boy does when he's thinking about something or somebody some place else. He lifted his free hand (the other being on the rubber grip of the motor's handle) and, with his forefinger, pointed to his own shirt pocket. We just looked into each other's eyes a minute, and for some reason I felt fine inside.

Then I swung my eyes around over the lake and in the direction of where the sun was going to set after awhile, and was glad I was alive—for the same reason Little Jim is glad he is alive.

In a little while, we'd be to shore. There was

only one thing about a fishing trip I didn't like and that was having to help clean the fish afterward, but boy oh boy, when you start sinking your teeth into the nice snow-white fish steaks, which restaurants' menus call *fillet,* you don't mind having had to clean them at all. Yum, yum, crunch, crunch . . . boy oh boy! I certainly was hungry. As our boat cut a wide circle and swung up beside the dock in front of our big brown tents, I could see that a fire was already started in the Indian kitchen we'd made. That meant that just the minute we had our fish cleaned Barry'd have them sizzling in the skillet for us.

Tom and I were alone a minute at the end of the dock that night just before we went to bed, and he had both hands clasped around the slender flagpole and was swaying his body forward and backward and sidewise not saying anything for a minute, and neither was I. Then he said, "I wish I could find my dad."

There was a tear in his voice and I knew he was feeling pretty awful inside, and because I liked him, I felt the same way for a minute.

"Nobody knows where he is," I said, and Tom surprised me by saying, "Only *one* Person knows. As quick as I realized what he meant, I said, "Yes, that's right. He knows everything in the world at the same time."

The moon shining on the water looked like it nearly always does in the moonlight—like silver—and like a field of oats on dad's farm would look if somebody had painted it white and the wind was blowing.

Santa, who, as you know, had his cabin not very far up the lake from where we were camped, had gone away for the night, and Big Jim and Circus had been selected to stay all night in his cabin to sort of look after things for him. They were the biggest members of our gang and Barry gave them permission.

All the rest of the gang were in the tents, maybe undressing, and Tom and I were really alone, when all of a sudden I heard a sound on the shore and a voice calling in a low husky whisper, "Tom! Hey—Tom!" And I was sure I had heard the voice before.

I saw the bushes part and a dark form move out in the moonlight, and at the same time Tom let go of the flagpole, and made a dive for the shore, beating it up the dock as fast as he could.

I was so surprised I couldn't move, but felt weak in the knees and sick at the stomach. Tom was there in a flash, and I watched him and somebody standing side by side, talking in whispers.

Then the dark form I'd seen come out of the bushes dived back again, and a second later I heard footsteps going lickety-sizzle up the lake shore. Then Tom started back to me and I met him in the middle of the dock.

"Who *was it?*" I said, thinking I knew. "Was it your dad?"

"No," Tom said, "it was my brother Bob. I gave him the letter from Mother, and he's going to give it to Dad."

8

CAN YOU IMAGINE THAT! Big Bob Till, Big Jim's worst enemy, and, except for Big Jim, the fiercest fighter in the whole country anywhere maybe! He was what people called a "juvenile delinquent," which means he was a bad boy who didn't like to behave himself and had done things that were against the law.

Maybe I'd better tell you right now, in case you don't know it, .that Mr. Foote, Little Jim's dad, had used his influence back at Sugar Creek to keep Bob from having to go to reform school. Then Bob had been what is called "paroled" to him, and Little Jim himself had been glad 'cause he'd rather anybody would be *good* than to have him be *bad* and have to be punished for it. But Bob was still not behaving himself, because he hadn't been trained at home like most of the rest of us. Even we were having a hard enough time to be even half as good as we thought we were, and we had had training all our boy lives.

When Tom said to me there in the moonlight

in the middle of the dock that he'd given his mom's letter to his brother Bob, and I realized that Bob was up here in the North Woods—in fact had been standing right over there behind those bushes only a second ago—you could have knocked me over with a moonbeam, I was so surprised. Of course, he was gone now—somewhere or other—but where?

I asked Tom a question then. "Where IS your dad?" And he said, "I don't know, but Bob does, and he'll take Mother's letter to him."

It seemed like the rest of the gang ought to know Bob was up here, and yet for some reason it seemed like Poetry ought to know it first. So the very second I had a chance after I got into my tent a little later, and the lights were out, and Dragonfly had been quieted down from talking and laughing—in fact, his noisy nose sounded like he was asleep—I reached out my hand and touched Poetry and said, "You asleep?" And he whispered quietly, "Yes," which meant he wasn't. So I told him about Bob and he said, "That explains a lot of things."

"What, for instance?" I asked, and he said, "It explains who opened the icehouse door and let John Till out." Then Poetry and I decided to get up and go outside where we could talk without being heard.

I was surprised we were able to get up and out without being stopped by Dragonfly's waking up and asking questions or insisting on going along. He is never able to let anybody have any secrets without wanting him to divide them up with *him*.

A good place to talk without being heard would be down at the dock, we decided, so away we went toward the lake where the waves were sighing and lapping against the shore and dock posts and making the boats rock a little. One of the boats made a little scraping noise against the dock.

"Where was Bob standing?" Poetry asked, and when I pointed to the bushes he started straight toward them. As you maybe know he wanted to be a detective some day and was always looking for what detectives and the police and the FBI call "clues"; and also Poetry was always finding one, or something he thought was one.

As soon as we were both behind the bushes, where nobody at camp could see us, he turned on his flashlight and shined it all around where Bob and Tom had been standing.

"What're we looking for?" I asked, and he answered like he always does, "A clue."

"What kind of a clue?" I asked, and he replied, "I'll tell you just as soon as I find it."

Well, I certainly didn't expect we'd find anything, but all of a sudden I heard a sound from up the shore like footsteps coming toward us, so I said in a husky whisper, "I think I *heard* a clue coming from somewhere." Up the path not very far away I saw a flashlight flash on and off.

We crouched low, hardly daring to breathe, knowing that somebody was coming for sure, and wondering who it was, and what he wanted. Was it Bob Till or maybe Old hook-nosed John Till himself?

Right that second, I saw something white lying where my feet had been a jiffy before. It looked like a folded white handkerchief or something, so I stooped down, reached out my hand to touch it, and it was an envelope of some kind.

"Little Tom's mom's letter," I thought. "Bob dropped it, and is coming back to look for it."

Poetry and I kept even quieter than we had been. He did not know, of course, what I'd just found and tucked into my pajama pocket. We had not taken time to dress but were in our pajamas—I in my green and white striped ones and Poetry in his purple ones.

It was a queer feeling we had, right that second. For some reason we decided to get ourselves out of there, which we did, sneaking back maybe fifteen feet before we decided to stop and wait to see who it was and what he was looking for and why, if we could.

In a few excited moments, whoever it was, was right where we ourselves had been, and was flashing his flashlight on and off, all around, right where a little while before I'd picked up the envelope. I could see he wasn't very tall—not as tall as Big John Till, so I decided it might be Bob again. Poetry had hold of my arm so tight it actually hurt, which showed, even though he was usually calm in a time of excitement, that this time he was pretty tense himself.

I certainly didn't know what to do, and would have been afraid to do it even if I had. Besides I wouldn't have had time to do much of anything, for right that second whoever it was, stopped searching and I heard his footsteps going on past, and in the direction of Santa's dock, which was several hundred yards farther on.

I remembered the envelope in my pocket and thought that it wasn't mine, and that I ought to call out to whoever it was, and say, "Hey, there, mister, whatever you're looking for, I've got it, whatever it is!" But I didn't. A little later, Poetry and I were alone with ourselves, and the only sound there was, was the friendly lapping of the waves against the dock posts and the washing of other waves against the sandy shore. Away out on the lake there was a great big shimmering silver spot of moonlight which was very pretty. Still farther was the shadow of the trees on the little island on the other side of which we had caught our walleye that afternoon and where Wally had lost his life. Right that minute he was maybe half digested in the stomach of a great big ugly-snouted northern pike.

I could feel my heart beating with excitement, but there was something else I was feeling too. It was the envelope I had in my pocket, which I quick took out. I whispered for Poetry to turn on his light, which he did, and this is what we saw on the envelope, written in pencil that was kinda smeared like pencil marks on a letter are when a boy has carried it around in his pocket or in his hands awhile. We saw written in a big awkward scrawl, the name *Bob Till*, but there wasn't anything else, not even an address—and no postage stamp.

Quick as anything, not stopping to think that that letter was private property and he had no right to open it, Poetry had the inside out of the envelope and was unfolding it, and I was holding his trembling flashlight on it to see what it said. And—would you believe it? It was a sheet of white typewriter paper and there wasn't a thing on it, not even a pencil mark.

"It's another invisible-ink map," Poetry said to me, and I remembered quick the other one we'd found. I told you about it in another story. When we'd warmed it up it had turned out to be a map of the territory up here, showing where the little kidnapped girl had been found, and which way the broken twig trails led. And we had followed them and finally found the ransom money in the old icehouse.

"And here's a *note*," Poetry whispered, as a little folded piece of paper with writing on it tumbled out.

That note, which was printed in pencil, said,

Dear Bob:
  Santa's away tonight. Get my boat which is tied to his dock and pick me up at the Indian cemetery at 10 o'clock and we'll get the rest of the ransom money. If I'm not there, wait till I come.

                    Your Dad

Well, when I saw what Poetry's trembling flashlight showed us written on that unfolded piece of paper, you could have knocked me over with a question mark, I was so surprised. Our mystery had come to life again and we were going to have another exciting adventure before our vacation was over. Hurrah! Boy oh boy!

Poetry spoke first, saying excitedly, "I'll bet Bob's going down to get the boat *right now*! We've got to stop him!"

"Why?" I said, and he said, "Stop him and make him tell us where his dad is. Then we or the police can capture him."

"Bob wouldn't tell us," I said, being sure he wouldn't.

"Well, for pity's sake, we must do *something*!" Poetry exclaimed to me. When I said, "What?" he said, "Get the gang and beat Bob to the cemetery!" That made as good sense as anything I could have thought of, especially since right that minute I heard an outboard motor somewhere and guessed that Bob had already started the powerful black-shrouded motor that was on the boat John Till had had, and which the police had left at Santa's dock.

We didn't have time to decide anything right then, though, 'cause almost as quick as a lightning bug can flash his flash on and off, we heard somebody running toward us from the direction of Santa's cottage. A second later, two forms came puffing out into the moonlight and into our camp. It was Big Jim and Circus, who, as you already know, were staying all night in Santa's cabin, just to sort of look after things for him.

I thought of Tom Till, and hated to have him

know what was going on, which he would if there was a lot of boy noise and the whole camp should wake up and come scrambling over each other down to the dock in crazy-looking pajamas, talking and wondering "What on earth?"

So Poetry and I shushed Big Jim and Circus and the four of us started to tell each other what we knew.

"Somebody took John Till's boat!" Circus puffed. "Hear him? There he goes now!"

About two hundred yards from shore I saw a shadow of a boat out in the moonlight and heard the roar of a powerful motor, and knew we'd have to hurry to get to the Indian cemetery first.

"Let's step on the gas and get going," Circus said as soon as we'd told them about the note we had found. Poetry asked, "What kind of gas— outboard motor, or station wagon?"

Big Jim, knowing that most of the Sugar Creek Gang had more bravery than good sense and that we sometimes did things that were dangerous, without thinking first, said, "This is another job for the police." But Poetry spoke up and said, "Let's be policemen ourselves. By the time we could phone them and they could get there, it'd be too late," which it would be, I thought. So we decided we ought to try to get to the cemetery first by driving there as fast as we could in the station wagon.

What to do about Tom was our first problem, but we wouldn't have much time to try to solve it. Some of us simply had to get going to the cemetery to be there before Bob could get to the Narrows, zip through them, and into that other lake where the cemetery was. It was half past nine right that second, and Bob was supposed to meet his dad there at ten. If only we could get there before either one of them did, and hide somewhere in the bushes. Then maybe we could sneak up on them, and get both of them at once—'cause it looked like Bob was in on the business of being a helper to the kidnapper too.

Barry and Little Jim were the only ones left in Barry's tent. Barry must have heard our excited talk, 'cause in a jiffy his tent flap plopped open and out he came and wanted to know what on earth all the excitement was all about. We told him and showed him the note and he also heard Bob's motor on the lake at the same time. We didn't stop to try to figure out why John Till had *written* to Bob instead of just *telling* him where to meet him, or anything. Right that minute almost, Little Jim and Tom came tumbling out of Barry's tent and in our direction, and Dragonfly came out of the other tent, and there we all were—too many—and some of us too little—to go on a kidnapper hunt.

I guess I never was so disappointed in my life as I was right that minute, though, 'cause Barry took charge of things quick. He said, "You boys all stay right here, and look after camp. I've a phone call to make—and I want to see the firewarden a minute."

"Is there a fire somewhere?" Tom Till asked quick, sniffing to see if anything smelled like smoke. And Dragonfly did the same thing, and sneezed just like he had actually smelled something he was allergic to.

A bit later, Barry in the station wagon was riding down the lane toward Santa's boathouse and I knew that in a few seconds he'd be pulling in low up a steep hill, swishing along a sandy trail at the top, and driving like mad down a winding road through the forest to the firewarden's house, which you know about if you've read *The Sugar Creek Gang Goes North*. There he'd make a terribly fast phone call to the police—or else let the firewarden's wife do it while he and the firewarden would beat it on to the Indian cemetery. They'd probably stop before they got there though, and sneak carefully up along the lake shore to where Bob's boat would be coming in, and, if they could, they'd capture both Bob and

101

John. I felt terribly disappointed inside, like I'd just blown up a very pretty great big colored balloon, and somebody had stuck a pin into it and it had burst. I didn't know there was going to be more excitement where we were than where Barry and the firewarden would be.

9

THE STATION WAGON hadn't any sooner disappeared and the whirring sound of its motor faded away, leaving us all with Barry's orders to go back to bed ringing in our ears, than I remembered the blank sheet of typewriter paper I had in my pocket and which we hadn't bothered to show to Barry.

Little Jim and Tom Till didn't know anything about what was going on, and they, being sleepy anyway, seemed glad to get back to their tent and make a dive back into the sleep from which they had dragged themselves a little while before.

Dragonfly was suspicious, though, and when he noticed Poetry and Big Jim and Circus and me talking together, he got a stubborn expression in his voice and aimed a question at us. "You guys got a secret of some kind?"

We didn't want him to start any fuss; besides sometimes he wasn't such a dumb person to let in on a secret. So for a little while we left Little Jim and Tom Till alone in their tent and the five of us went into the other tent, lit a lantern, unfolded the piece of typewriter paper and heated it over the hot top of the lantern. In only a few minutes we were looking at a map of the territory up here—showing the camp where we were and the place where the little Ostberg girl had been lying, just like the other map we'd found. Also different other places were identified, such as Santa's boathouse, the firewarden's cabin, and the broken twig trail which led off in different directions.

"Both maps are alike," Circus said, and it looked like they were. Poetry traced the faint markings of the new one with his pencil so we could study it better.

"What do you suppose Bob had two maps for?" Dragonfly asked, and Poetry answered by saying, "He maybe had only one at first, but when he lost it—the one we found last week—he or Hooknose made another one."

"Yeah," I said, with a questionmark in my voice, "but why draw them in invisible ink?"

"Maybe so nobody would think they were maps."

"But how could Bob *himself* know the different places if he couldn't see the lines and different marks?" I asked, wondering how.

It was Dragonfly who answered my doubt by

saying, "Oh, he probably had what they call an 'original'—and as soon as he'd memorized it, he drew another one in invisible ink and tore the first one up!" His idea made sense, I thought, and said so, and so did Poetry.

Well, we weren't getting anywhere—and weren't supposed to anyway. It certainly didn't seem fair to us that Barry hadn't let us go with him, but he was camp boss and that was that, and we were supposed to crawl back into our sleeping bags and go to sleep. Imagine that! Right while Barry and the firewarden, and maybe the police, were capturing Old hook-nosed John Till and his son Bob! *Imagine* it! It was terribly disappointing.

And then all of a sudden Dragonfly gasped and said, "Hey, Gang! Look!" He had the newest map and was holding it up between his dragonfly-like eyes and the light. His voice had contagious excitement in it, so we all looked quick to see what he saw. But it wasn't anything—only two crude-looking fish away off on the part of the map which was supposed to represent a lake.

"A couple of fish," I said, disgusted with him for getting us excited over nothing. "That's to show you there is a lake there."

"Yeah," he said, still excited, "but look where they *are*! They're right over there where that island is where we caught our walleye today."

105

Big Jim answered by saying, "Maybe they're supposed to locate a good fishing place."

And then Dragonfly got another idea which sent our minds whirling like summer cyclones at Sugar Creek, when he said, "You know what that is? That's where the island is, and that's where John Till has been catching the big fish to put the ransom money in, and that island's where maybe the rest of the money is right this very minute. I'll bet that's where they'll go to get the rest of it, if Barry or the police don't catch 'em first!"

Well, sir, you could have knocked me over with an invisible ink map, when Dragonfly gave us that wonderful idea. It seemed like he was exactly right, and it seemed a shame that I hadn't thought of it first—in fact, for a minute it almost seemed like I had, because all of a sudden I was remembering what I'd thought in the afternoon when Poetry and I had been exploring that island looking for clues. Also I remembered that that island is where I'd wanted to go to start hunting for the treasure in the first place when I'd thought of playing Robinson Crusoe and his Man Friday and also Treasure Island. I just knew that Dragonfly and I were right, so as quick as a flash I said, "If we really want to capture Bob and Old Hook-nose, we'd better beat it over to that little island, and be hiding there somewhere when they get there, and capture them ourselves."

Big Jim answered me in a tone of voice that sounded like he thought I was only about half bright when he said, "Who wants to get the living daylights knocked out of him in the middle of the night? When you saw him the *first* time, didn't he have a big hunting knife?"

I remembered he had—in fact, in my mind's eye, I could still see that wicked looking knife with its five-inch-long blade that looked like it could not only make a quick slice into the stomach of a fish but could do the same thing to a boy. When Big Jim said that to me like that, it seemed like maybe he was right and I was very ignorant for wanting to be brave without using good sense.

"Besides," Big Jim said, "those two silly looking fish out there on the map don't mean a thing. We'd better all get some sleep or we'll be as tired as wrung-out dishrags tomorrow."

Well, that was orders, and a boy is supposed to obey anybody who has a right to be his boss— such as a schoolteacher or a camp leader or either one of his parents, or somebody he is working for. Big Jim didn't always get obeyed, though, because our gang nearly always voted on important things to decide what to do. So right away Poetry, who thought my idea wasn't so bad after all, spoke up and said, "I move we all get into Barry's big boat and go roaring over to that island, beach the boat on the sandy shore of the cove behind some willows and be there waiting when Bob and Hook-nose come—if they do."

"Second the motion," I said quick, but Big Jim exploded our idea by saying, "It's *Barry's* orders to go to bed."

It certainly wasn't easy to go to bed when there was so much excitement we'd rather be mixed up in, but orders were orders, so pretty soon I was in my sleeping bag in the same tent with Dragonfly and Poetry. Big Jim and Circus had decided to go back to Santa's cabin to spend the rest of the night like they'd planned to in the first place.

Pretty soon, in spite of feeling excited and wondering whether anybody would catch Old John Till and his son Bob, I dropped off to sleep—not even knowing I was going to do it. A certain poem says, "No boy knows when he goes to sleep." It seemed like even in my sleep I could hear an outboard motor roaring out on the lake, first coming close to us, then fading away and then a little later coming back again.

Once when I was half awake and half asleep, I heard Poetry turn over beside me and then I heard him whisper, "Bill—listen, will you? Somebody's out there in a motor boat going back and forth in front of our dock."

It took a while for me to realize where I was, and why, and then I was actually listening to an outboard motor away out on our lake like somebody was doing what Poetry said he was.

A second later, Poetry sat up, scrambled over to the tent flap, worked it open, and in another second I had my red head beside his, and we were both looking out across the moonlit water, and seeing a dark fast-moving boat out there.

"The crazy goof!" Poetry said to me in my left ear, and I said to him in his right one, "He's cutting big wide circles."

It seemed silly for anybody to do what he was doing; so, because it was a crazy night anyway, and so many odd things had happened on our fishing trip, Poetry and I squeezed our way through the tent flap and went down to the dock to see what on earth anybody was doing out there going round and round like that. And then all of a sudden, Poetry gasped excitedly and said, "Hey, *there isn't anybody in that boat. It's empty!*"

Just that second the boat came out into the middle of a big wide silver path which lakes have on moonlight nights, when you look out across them in the direction of the moon. And sure enough, Poetry was right. I could hardly believe my surprised eyes, but in that silver path was a row boat about the size of the one Bob Till had gone away in, cutting big, terribly fast wide circles, going round and round and round. The motor sounded exactly like the big black-shrouded two-cylinder one I knew how to run so well and which Bob had taken from Santa's dock.

It didn't make sense—a boat out there without anybody in it.

"Hey, it's getting *closer*! The wind is blowing it toward the shore. It gets closer every time it makes a circle!"

What to do or whether to do anything, was the question. Poetry and I stood there on the dock in our pajamas, not slapping at the mosquitoes, because when the wind blows, like it was right that second, mosquitoes' smallish wings can't control their flight, and they stop looking for boys to bite.

Whirr! . . . *roar!* . . . *whizz* . . . and also *plop!* . . . *plop!* . . . *plop!* The motor was doing the whirring and the whizzing, and the bottom of the boat was doing the plopping on the waves.

"It's empty!" we said to each other, and it looked like it was, for sure.

"Maybe whoever was in it fell out. Maybe it was John Till and he was drunk and fell out and the boat just keeps on running," I said. I knew a motor could do that, and if the steering handle was set, it would maybe stay set, and the motor would keep on going until it ran out of gas, or until it rammed into an island or a shore somewhere. Then that boat straightened out a little, like the motor's steering handle had swung around —which they do sometimes when nobody holds onto them—and the boat came roaring straight toward our dock at a terrific rate of speed. In another half minute it would crash into the end of the dock where we were—right there by the flagpole. It was coming toward us as straight as a torpedo and almost as fast, I thought, as though this was a war and somebody had shot a torpedo straight for where we were.

And then, a second later while my mind was whirling, not believing it could or would happen, the sharp prow of that big white boat with the fierce racing motor on the other end of it struck with a crash that jarred and shook the dock, glanced sidewise, swerved up along its edge and ran into the sandy shore. At the same time, or just before, the propeller, down in the water, struck the shallow sandy bottom, which made the motor tilt forward.

The motor made a couple of ridiculous-sounding discouraged sneezes and coughs, and stopped.

Then almost before the sound of the crash had stopped splitting my eardrums, I was over near the boat, looking down into it and shining my flashlight into it. There lying in the bottom was a great big quart-sized whiskey bottle, and my imagination told me that maybe John Till had been in the boat and that he had gotten drunk and had fallen out and was out there in the lake somewhere already drowned. My heart sank as I thought of what a hurt heart Little Tom Till would have when he found it out.

The waves of the lake were splashing against the dock post and lapping at the shore and the boat, and I knew it was a terribly tense minute. And then Poetry, who was beside me, grabbed my arm like he had just heard something terribly important, and said, "Listen . . . SH! . . . *Listen!*"

I listened, and didn't hear anything at first, and then all of a sudden I did, and it was a scared voice calling from somewhere crying, "HELP . . . HELP . . . !"

10

I CERTAINLY DIDN'T DREAM that things were going to turn out the way they did when that mad boat came racing toward us and whammed itself into our dock and up onto the shore and turned partway over on its side, and we heard a voice calling from somewhere, "HELP . . . HELP . . . HELP!" The first thing I thought of was that somebody, I didn't know who, was out there somewhere drowning and had to have help right away quick. Santa's house was several hundred yards up the shore, and any yelling I or any of us could have done for Big Jim and Circus to come and help us couldn't have been heard by them. And by the time any of us could have run up there and wakened them, it would have been too late to save whoever's life needed to be saved.

Quick as anything, I said to Poetry, "We've got to do something or maybe somebody will drown out there!"

But say, I didn't have to tell Poetry to step

on the gas to get going. He was the fastest-acting barrel-shaped boy you ever saw. In less time than it takes me to write it for you, Poetry had quick picked up two oars that were lying there and tossed them into a row boat that was on the opposite side of the dock, and in an instant was unwinding the anchor rope from around the dock post. Then he yelled to me, "Hurry up and get in quick, and get the oars into the oarlocks, and let's row out quick and save him."

Even while we were making a lot of noise, it seemed I could still hear that voice out there calling, "HELP . . . HELP . . . H-E-L-P!"

We got the boat's prow headed into the waves, which is what you have to do when you row on a lake—keep the prow headed toward the oncoming waves, or you'll maybe get your boat filled with water.

Right that minute I heard another yell coming from the direction of the tents, and it was Dragonfly racing toward us in flapping pajamas wanting to know what on earth was going on and why.

I yelled back to him from the boat I was already in, and said, "Hey, you—Dragonfly! Beat it down to Santa's cabin and tell Big Jim and Circus to step on the gas and get Santa's motor boat and come out to help us! There's somebody drowning out there in the moonlight!"

As quick as anything, Poetry and I were on our way. Our boat had three life-preserver cushions in it—enough for Poetry and me and whoever was out there, which of course had to be John Till, I thought, on account of the whiskey bottle in the bottom of the boat that had just roared its way up onto our shore.

If our own boat should upset or something, and we were tossed out into the water, we could swim to our cushions and by keeping our bodies down under the water and holding onto the cushions for dear life, we could manage to keep our faces above water, and the cushions would hold us up.

Poetry and I sat in the middle seat, side by side, with Poetry sitting nearer the center than I so our boat would be well balanced, on account of he was a whole lot heavier than I was. Each one of us used an oar and we rowed as fast as we could in the direction the call for HELP had come from.

Our oars made a squeaking noise in the locks and the blades made a little splashing sound in the water, and also the waves plopping against the prow of the boat made it hard for us to hear the call for help, and also hard to tell just which direction to go. But we kept on rowing hard, and I could see the shore getting farther and farther away. For a jiffy I was glad that my parents had taught me how to work on the farm and that I had muscles that sometimes felt as strong as the muscles of the man in a poem Poetry is always quoting, "The Village Blacksmith," which goes,

> Under the spreading chestnut tree
> The village smithy stands,
> The smith—a mighty man is he,
> With large and sinewy hands,
> And the muscles of his brawny arms
> Are strong as iron bands.

But even though my arm muscles felt that strong, my knees felt sort of weak as I realized that a man's life was depending on us. We kept on rowing as hard and as fast as we could, grunting and sweating and hoping, and also doing what any boy with good sense, or even without it, would do at a time like that—*praying* as hard as anything. Anyway I was, and I was asking God to please help us get there quick—for when a boy is in the middle of such a dangerous excitement as I was in, he will ask God to help him even though he hasn't been a very good boy and isn't sure God will have anything to do with him. I tell you, all of a sudden, I was thinking of Little Tom and his swell mother and it just seemed like it would be terrible for them to lose their dad, even if he was maybe the meanest man that ever lived at Sugar Creek.

Another reason I was praying with every grunt was that I knew John Till wasn't a Christian and if he didn't become one before he died, he'd never get to go to heaven, because my parents had told me the Bible says, "Except a man be born again, he cannot see the kingdom of God." Anybody who knows what Dad calls the "ABC's of the Gospel" knows that you can be born again just by letting the Saviour into your heart, but John Till had never done that.

I guess maybe I didn't use any words with my prayer, though, but only some worried thoughts, which I sort of shot up to heaven as quick as I could, like I shoot arrows with my bow when I'm back home around Sugar Creek. In fact, for a while it seemed like I was shooting prayer-arrows up to God, and that on the end of each one, instead of a little feather, I had written a note on a strip of paper. And on each note it said, "Please, Heavenly Father, Old John Till's soul is lost, and if he drowns without being saved, it'll be terrible. Help us get to him quick."

Then Poetry interrupted my thoughts saying, "Stop a minute—LISTEN!"

I let my oar rest for a moment, and right away the waves made our boat swerve a little, like it

117

would swing around if we didn't keep on rowing. But I heard a voice not more than fifty feet farther on, and looking quick, I saw something dark in the water, struggling. And the voice with a desperate gasp cried, "Hurry—I—HELP!" Then it stopped.

I tell you we hurried and I kept on sending up arrows—grunting and pulling and wishing. Then without knowing I was going to say it, I said, "O please don't let him drown. 'Cause Poetry and I have got a secret about one of Your Bible verses, that says if two of us agree on something we ask for, You will answer us."

It just seemed like maybe John Till had to be saved, on account of it seemed like that promise in the Bible was especially about him. Then without knowing I was going to say it aloud, I said, "And here comes another arrow with the same thing written on it," and Poetry beside me said, "What arrow? What are you talking about?"

I explained it to him, while we rowed harder, and even though he didn't say much, I knew he was doing the same thing I was. My parents had taught me to pray when I was little, and I still liked to, even though my folks sometimes might wonder if I ever did or not, because I was sometimes too mischevious. Also sometimes I wasn't always what they called a "good boy," which is an expression they use when they mean I ought to behave myself.

In another second we were close to John Till, and I noticed it was really him, and he didn't have any life preserver pillow. He had probably been drunk and had just tumbled out of his boat while it was racing terribly fast, and had been swimming ever since.

I quick grabbed up a cushion in front of my feet and with a wide sweep of my arm tossed it out toward him. My aim was as good as David's had been when he had used his sling shot on the giant that time in the Bible. The pillow landed with a ker-plop right in front of Old John and I saw him make a fierce desperate lunge toward it and grab hold of it with both arms and heard him yell in a sputtering voice something I never dreamed I'd hear from Old John Till's voice that night. It was, *"Thank God, I'm saved!"*

Then he quit trying to swim and just lay back on his back, and held onto the cushion and let himself float, with only his face above water with the cushion in front of his chin. That is the way to float, if you ever have to hold onto a life-preserver cushion.

In a moment we had our boat there, and Old John was crying and gasping and saying, "Thank God—Oh, thank you, boys, thank you!"

How to get him into the boat was the question, though, for the minute he would try to get in, his heavy weight might tip us over.

But say, in spite of being exhausted and gasping for breath, Old John Till still had good sense, and didn't try to climb in right away, but got his breath first. Besides, in a minute Circus and Big Jim with Dragonfly holding a flashlight to help them see us, came motoring out. In a little while we had John in the boat, and we were all on our way to shore, with John so tired out he just laid his terribly wet self down and sort of shook and sniffled and half cried while we moved along.

I tell you it's a wonderful feeling when you've done something like that. You're glad not only 'cause you helped do it, but if you believe what Poetry and I believed, you feel like you and the heavenly Father are very good friends—which is maybe the best feeling a boy ever has.

As we rowed along toward shore, Old John just lay in the bottom of the boat like a terribly big wet fish that had just been caught, and was so tired out he couldn't move. Pretty soon, Poetry whispered, "Do you think he's pretending to be good—and that he just said those religious words back there, to fool us, and is maybe playing possum? Do you think when we get to shore he'll quick make a dive for the bushes and run away?"

I'd seen possums act like that back home. They were lively until they were caught, then they would do what is called "play possum"—just roll over on their sides and curl up into a half circle and shut their eyes and act dead until we or the dogs went away a few yards. Then they would come to quick life, scramble to their ridiculous feet that look like hands, and run to a tree and climb up it or to a hole in the ground and dive into it.

"I don't know," I said to Poetry, "but he sounded like he meant what he said when he said those words back there." I wanted to believe it, 'cause I wanted Tom Till to have a brand new dad like Circus had gotten when his dad had been saved a couple of years before.

Well, it turned out that I was right. That whiskey bottle we'd seen in the bottom of his boat hadn't had whiskey in it at all, but was one Little Jim had put a gospel tract in. Old John had found it and read it, and the Lord Himself had used it to do what our Sugar Creek minister calls, "convict him of his sins." On top of that, he had also stopped to read the message in the other whiskey bottle which had been used as a marker for a good crappie-fishing place out in front of the Indian cemetery. Also he had been listening on his portable radio to the radio program of the Church of the Cross. So, after he had accidentally tumbled out of the boat tonight, he'd gotten half scared to death, and all the verses of the Bible and the sermons he had read and listened to, came splashing into his mind. And without stopping to think that he didn't believe in God, he had prayed to Him to not only save his body from drowning, but to save his *soul* from being lost.

When we rescued him, he had the other $5,000 of the ransom money in his trousers pocket. It was pretty wet, but as good as gold. And—do you know what? He told us he hadn't been helping the real kidnapper at all, but had only wanted to get the $1,000 reward!

"And now, boys," John's gruff, trembling voice said, as we listened to him explain things, "you'll have to start praying for Bob—we had a quarrel tonight, and he's gone away somewhere."

"Where?" Tom Till spoke up and asked. All of us were sitting around a camp fire which we'd started quick, to get John warmed up after we'd got some of Barry's dry clothes on him, and a blanket wrapped around him. Most of the rest of us were wrapped in blankets too.

John looked down at his red-haired, freckled-faced, trembling-voiced boy, and said, "I don't know. I—he thought we ought to keep the $5,000 instead of turning it in. I—I'm afraid I was too hard on him, maybe. But when we couldn't agree about this $5,000, I took the boat and left him there at the Indian cemetery."

We asked Old John different questions, one of them being, "How'd you know where the ransom money was?" And he said, "I studied the newspapers and the pictures, and found the kidnapper's map in the grave-house of an old Indian chief. I made two copies in invisible ink—one for myself and the other for Bob, but I lost mine somewhere—and you boys found it."

"But why, if you only wanted the $1,000 reward, did you bury the money in the fish in the ice-house?" we asked him.

"I didn't," he said, just as Little Tom Till shoved a stick into the fire and about a thousand yellow sparks shot in different directions up toward the sky. "Old Brains Powers, the kidnapper, buried it there. I'd been digging it up. I had five thousand dollars already dug up, and was coming back to get the rest of it, but you boys beat me to it. Then when I went into the icehouse, you slammed the door on me and barred it, and I would have stayed there until the police came, but Bob, who had just gotten up here, heard me hollering and let me out."

Poetry spoke up and said, with a doubt in his voice, "If you were only after the money so you could get the reward for finding it, why did you run away?"

"I was afraid the police wouldn't believe my story."

Well, there is the whole mystery untangled for you, and a wonderful camping trip all over for another year. Boy oh boy! I hope I get to go again next year—if not to the same place, then up to Canada or somewhere where there will be even more exciting adventures than there were this year.

But before that happens there'll be a whole year full of different things that will happen back home at Sugar Creek. I just know that something terribly interesting *will* happen to us before another summer rolls around. In fact, there was a letter from my folks in our mail box at the dock the very day we left camp, saying, "We'll be looking for you, Bill—and do we ever have interesting news for you! Don't try to guess what it is—'cause you can't."

And—well, all the way home in our station wagon, I did just what my parents told me not to—I kept trying to guess what the interesting news would be.